ABOUT CREATION

WHO WE ARE

An Inquiry of Human Being
By
Bob Demyanovich

For the gifted lives of our occupation

Scripture References cited in this book are from the Old and New Testaments of the
King James Version of the Bible

About Creation
Title ID: 3756556
ISBN-13: 978-0615584188

Preface

Curiosity usually manages to slip past caution hoping to look beyond the easy answer or peril to obtain what may be known of the entirety. About Creation confirms the introductory role of curiosity touching the essence of human being. Studies and investigation of the world we inhabit conclude that natural selection continued an evolution into our peculiar species, the human experience. Science seeks to prove how life arrives. The creator God is another choice to explain our being. The Judeo Christian Bible prompted meditation, prayer, and study for multitudes over centuries. Philosophers, scholars, and governments have pondered both evolution and biblical creation seeking an explanation for our existence. Every human considers and evaluates the reason for their life within the societies of their residence. Contemplation of our being will review evolution and the biblical account because they are repositories of explanations for us. Observations and quotations within this study are not rare, unique or new discoveries unknown in common learning and experiences. This ubiquitous commonality however must exude a type of hypnotic dullness, a mistaken confidence to account for behaviors and pronouncements circulating in our societies today. Apparently the gravity of the reason for our being and investigative opportunity are blunted and displaced by concerns for acquisition, family, business, government, residence or even preoccupation with products of recreation. When do people become aware that an era of transformation has overtaken them?

Who are we? What are we? Why are we here? Questions such as these crave motive or vindication for our very existence. Upon this wonderment we are wholly malleable. Answers have been, are and will be offered yet elements of such absolute control must be recognized as such. The selection of either purposeful creation or a natural occurrence of our being provides undergirding guidance to the conduct of our personal and interpersonal living. This elemental component for human conduct is the heart of contention and so the question of who we are remains unresolved. Our accustomed living, our experience occurs at the moment of indecision between these two belief structures intent to direct the conclusions and compulsions for our lives. Avoidance of this caustic issue does not afford sanctuary. Consider your personal wellbeing in a world populated through natural selection. Moral conduct quite likely would be replaced with truce pacts among power players where civility would be conditional. Personal and national restraint that tests motive or withstands a purpose would be loosened or lost, evidenced by historical despots. Evolution is purported to occur as the physical conditions of existence eliminate the incapable. The terrible gravity of choice is not the primary creative agent in an evolutionary process. The purpose and value of existence within evolution then is tenuous. Any manner of conduct could be excused to adjust for a preferred result or for culling the inefficient. Human being contradicts evolution. Shock and dismay replace peace when cultural underpinnings are changed.

In an era engorged with opinions and conjecture potential is soon realized, this energy generates change. The new way arises untested but refreshing and attuned to the moment. None care to be identified with the refuse to be left behind or as reluctant to let ingenuity have free reign so comes the call for change. Care must be exercised in this spring awakening to seek and cultivate in good ground. Conjecture, fiction and imagination awaken our creative considerations for growth and enhancement but unless these moments are harnessed the expansion becomes a dispersion or dissolution.

Archeological discovery and technological enhancement provide a type of information. Historical records contain another type of information. Careful review of these sources is necessary to help part the curtains of time. This book is a consideration of an historical record. In order to obtain the intent of this historical record it comprises most of the text. This historical record asserts that it is exclusively true and hence is objectionable for at least 67% of the world population.

Contested subjects, especially controversial records acquire reputations that differ from the content as centuries pass beyond the events.

We ponder our existence, our purpose individually, socially and through our race consciousness. Culture and science attest to this questing. The study within this book contemplates human being, the lost being and the mystery of God. Surprisingly, the bible, that hoary book is now more contemporary than humanity is willing to admit. True enlightenment is startling, a foreboding realized in a headlong plunge snapping the cord of complacency. The bible is the book of human creation. The end of time, the end of human creation is declared in the last book of the bible. Biblical passages relating to conditions at the end of time were too fabulous for many to believe until the arrival of our modern era. Human being is in the creation process, the opportunity for emergence of spirit from the ordeal of flesh and death. This absolutely is a personal process. Creation is occurring right now in our very lives. The answer to the philosopher's quest is knowable. Choice is the meaning of life.

Table of Contents

2Cr 2:16 To the one [we are] the savour of death unto death; and to the other the savour of life unto life. And who [is] sufficient for these things?

Chapter 1
Who We Are

Who are we? Each of us has been exposed to this question as we began to consciously interrelate within society. Most people develop a self-appraisal sufficient to manage the "Who am I" question but the species identity is incomplete. We are the piece from some other puzzle. Humans are different than all other earthly life. We are the drama in this world prone to reactive sweeps of activity. Our lives would be grossly affected should either evolution or biblical revelation be verified as the actual account for our presence. The most familiar faces would become strangers if our true origin were ever discovered. We would look on each other with a new awareness and reorder our lives. Research has arrived at the theory of evolution to explain our presence. The bible explains our presence through revelation. Each tests the strength of our choice. Either one is an act of faith. You and I have already chosen between the two and order our lives accordingly. Read on friend, your life depends on it.

Was early human thought sufficient to create a story that manipulates even today? Was it only a mere slice of people throughout history that were much more intelligent than most of humanity? Were brute humans evolving, thinking, attaining society and culture through accretion to become who we are now or was profound ancient thought revealed by archeological evidences the actual condition? Has there been an ebb and tide of knowledge and society? Are theories of ancient humans accurately conceived apart from present day expectations or as constrained to fit an evolutionary model? Are we more aware today or merely deluded? So much irony in the reality of our being taunts conclusions of how we are who we are.

Is the biblical version of creation contained in the book of Genesis a fictional story? Might it be an opportunistic scenario that is claimed to be reliably transmitted through oral tradition but actually, is only a more palatable alternative than pantheistic lore?   Then is it just a story that renders believers predisposed for manipulation? A story as the atheists claim that in the beginning man created God? Is it a compilation of wisdom conveyed through an epic story structure? Is it a metaphorical rendition of original sin to manage the exclusive occurrence of human awareness?   Can it now be a substitute espousing a nobler explanation for humanity than merely as a consequence of the wandering course of evolution?   Or is it actually a revelation from God otherwise exclusive and unknowable to anyone but the creator? Consider this enigmatic book that purports a very startling view of humanity's inception. Contained therein is the evident interruption of common communion between God and humans.

Gen 3:8 And they heard the voice of the LORD God walking in the garden in the cool of the day: and Adam and his wife hid themselves from the presence of the LORD God amongst the trees of the garden. Gen 3:9 And the LORD God called unto Adam, and said unto him, Where [art] thou?

Darkness is no impediment to the creator, God. Does it seem questionable that God could not see Adam and Eve?   Nothing would be hidden from the creator. Biblically God gave them pause emphasizing the conditions at their transgression living the earliest moments within the process of creation, in the crucible and tension of possibilities, our own ancestor prototype.

Gen 1:2 And the earth was without form, and void; and darkness [was] upon the face of the deep. And the Spirit of God moved upon the face of the waters.

Gen 1:3 And God said, Let there be light: and there was light.
Psa 139:12 Yea, the darkness hideth not from thee; but the night shineth as the day: the darkness and the light [are] both alike [to thee].
2Ch 6:30 Then hear thou from heaven thy dwelling place, and forgive, and render unto every man according unto all his ways, whose heart thou knowest; (for thou only knowest the hearts of the children of men:)
Hbr 4:13 Neither is there any creature that is not manifest in his sight: but all things [are] naked and opened unto the eyes of him with whom we have to do.

The biblical first humans, Adam and Eve succumbed to temptation creating an existence apart from their creator thereby altering the totality of human being. Adam and Eve hid from God. Disobedience exhibits this behavior in those who are accountable to higher authority. In the evolutionary process physical conditions eliminate the incapable apart from choice. Evolution is not willful it is spontaneous. Evolutionary development does not rationalize the terrible gravity of choice, it is not involved. Opinions conceived within an evolutionary conception of being are blunted to choice, to responsibility.

Are Adam and Eve merely the x and y variable names for the set containing all humans or did they actually exist? Science has revealed bacteria, viruses and atomic structure. Science has comforted our lives, discovered the way of planets in our solar system and seeks to reveal secrets of the universe. Science is determined to plumb anything imagined from the micro to the macrocosm. Science however has not been sufficient to rescue evolution from theory. In the Genesis lineage, people are identified personally by name with the number of years they lived such as Adam, Seth, Enos, Cainan etc. Science provides theories with archeological discoveries,

DNA analysis and carbon dating whereas biblical persons link hands to provide a lineage forward from Adam and Eve.

Gen 5:4 And the days of Adam after he had begotten Seth were eight hundred years: and he begat sons and daughters:
Gen 5:5 And all the days that Adam lived were nine hundred and thirty years: and he died.
Gen 5:6 And Seth lived an hundred and five years, and begat Enos:
Gen 5:7 And Seth lived after he begat Enos eight hundred and seven years, and begat sons and daughters:

Beings with such long lives would be very powerful not only due to robust physiques but also by an exponention of knowledge fortified through so many more ages than our own lifetimes. These beings would be quite different than our own experience, they were phenomenal beings. Pride had too much incentive for the pre-flood inhabitants of our world so longevity was significantly reduced in the biblical account of human history.

Gen 6:3 And the LORD said, My spirit shall not always strive with man, for that he also [is] flesh: yet his days shall be an hundred and twenty years.

What would Adam and Eve have thought while in the garden? Were Adam and Eve's perceptions less sensorial and more spiritually attuned before their first sin? They had no want, the garden was theirs. Was their experience a melding of spirit and flesh? They were created from the dust of the ground and imbued with the breath of life how did their new minds perceive? How much knowing was imparted at their creation? First humans, there was no human fore bearer constraint to their decisions. They were truly the children of God. But biblically we are their children, contain their legacy and are the product of their choices. Are we a study of the course of thought? The human experience is a limiting condition suitable for a test of character or apprenticeship.

Rom 8:5 For they that are after the flesh do mind the things of the flesh; but they that are after the Spirit the things of the Spirit.
Gal 4:1 Now I say, [That] the heir, as long as he is a child, differeth nothing from a servant, though he be lord of all;
Gal 4:2   But is under tutors and governors until the time appointed of the father.
Gal 4:3   Even so we, when we were children, were in bondage under the elements of the world:
1Cr 15:46 Howbeit that [was] not first which is spiritual, but that which is natural; and afterward that which is spiritual.

Since our experience is primarily physical how is it that we acknowledge a spiritual existence? Do we actually perceive more than our five senses deliver? Our sensory lives do not accept the biblical insistence of spiritual preeminence. From the comfort of advanced cultures to the bare subsistence of the primitive our interaction, our communion transpires in the physical world. Yet we hope for better and when we have a lapse from our attention sponges we think that there is more to existence than what we see as we are about our world. What is this awareness that weighs our perceptions, our decisions and contemplates the wonder of our lives? We miss the lost component of our being, that quality that does not occur and cannot be found in the physical world.

1Cr 2:14 But the natural man receiveth not the things of the Spirit of God: for they are foolishness unto him: neither can he know [them], because they are spiritually discerned.

Who and What are We?

Laws, codes of conduct and belief structures develop to ensure the general good and welfare of human societies. One type of belief structure is most volatile. Beliefs involving the source of humanity are unverifiable and consequently contestable. Discovery of the source of humanity would alter all laws, codes and beliefs. A sensible approach seeks answers from physical evidence yet conclusions offered from insufficient information are a type of belief and arise from the proponents' own concept of existence.

Belief arising from the accumulated physical evidences must struggle to account for traits uniquely human without occurrence in any animal group. Conversely, belief from revelation offers answers purported to be from the source of generation. Revelation involves spiritual concepts that are inexplicable before belief is exercised in behavior. Humanity cannot prove that there is life beyond our common experience. The absence or existence of life after death is unattainable to human proof. How would matters of spirit be conveyed to physical beings?

Plants, insects and animals coexist yet these existences are unconcerned with other species and many have no regard for their own kind. These are then examples of existence unrecognized by cohabiters of the same environment. Humans exist in this same biosphere yet our awareness, unlike any other recognizes the interaction of phylum, genus, species etc. Human life is not an expression of the colony or hive but personal and resistant to compulsion. According to biblical revelation there is a superior awareness and supernatural existence.

Jhn 14:17 [Even] the Spirit of truth; whom the world cannot receive, because it seeth him not, neither knoweth him: but ye know him; for he dwelleth with you, and shall be in you.

Luk 10:21 In that hour Jesus rejoiced in spirit, and said, I thank thee, O Father, Lord of heaven and earth, that thou hast hid these things from the wise and prudent, and hast revealed them unto babes: even so, Father; for so it seemed good in thy sight.
Mat 16:1 The Pharisees also with the Sadducees came, and tempting desired him that he would shew them a sign from heaven.
Mat 16:2 He answered and said unto them, when it is evening, ye say, [It will be] fair weather: for the sky is red.
Mat 16:3 and in the morning, [It will be] foul weather to day: for the sky is red and lowring. O [ye] hypocrites, ye can discern the face of the sky; but can ye not [discern] the signs of the times?
Mat 16:4 A wicked and adulterous generation seeketh after a sign; and there shall no sign be given unto it, but the sign of the prophet Jonas. And he left them, and departed.
1Cr 1:22 For the Jews require a sign, and the Greeks seek after wisdom:

Biblical revelation presents concepts contrary to our physical experiences and unverifiable by laboratory analysis. Absent proof human motivation is laid bare. Our species centric righteousness clashes with God's biblical disappointment in humanity but there is no other comparator affording a non-human witness.

Isa 55:8 For my thoughts [are] not your thoughts, neither [are] your ways my ways, saith the LORD.
Rom 3:10 As it is written, There is none righteous, no, not one:
Rom 3:11 There is none that understandeth, there is none that seeketh after God.

Rom 3:12 They are all gone out of the way, they are together become unprofitable; there is none that doeth good, no, not one.
Mar 10:18 And Jesus said unto him, Why callest thou me good? [there is] none good but one, [that is], God. And Matt 19:17, Luke 18:19

Without an independent assessment by some other non-human reasoning species the bible beginning with creation and the genesis of humans is herein contemplated with the query into, "WHO and WHAT ARE WE"? Set apart from substantive facts of the beginning our lives exist at a perfect contest. We do choose during the course of our lives between physical or spiritual, God or humanism. Is biblical revelation comingled with consciousness of love, desire, intention and labor, personalized in chapters of life and death our own edenic contest?

Where to Begin

Investigation of our origin is challenged for the paucity of information of the time before humanity left durable history or, perhaps not. Genesis is quite specific regarding lineage and lifespan but history apart from the biblical record is disconnected.

Gen 9:28 And Noah lived after the flood three hundred and fifty years.
Gen 9:29 And all the days of Noah were nine hundred and fifty years: and he died.
Mat 1:17 So all the generations from Abraham to David [are] fourteen generations; and from David until the carrying away into Babylon [are] fourteen generations; and from the carrying away into Babylon unto Christ [are] fourteen generations.

14

Verse 17 of the first chapter of Matthew sums up the list of names from Abraham to Jesus in the preceding 15 verses. The fifth chapter of Genesis lists the pre Abraham names of people and their lifespan. The lineage from Jesus back to Adam is also listed in Luke 3:23 through 3:38.

Doubtless the passage of centuries erases any but the most determined effort to preserve an intact historical record. Ancient samples of the capability to express information by written figures in order to commit events to posterity occur in various forms from pictures to organized symbols and structure. Edifices and devices convey or document information in another manner. There are levels of sophistication among societies even today where some have nothing more than oral tradition. Do these evidences align to indicate an evolution or are the various examples isolated fruits of cultural choices and perceptions? Sparse effort is committed to preserving history in the course of individual lives. This behavior is not sufficiently addressed in current theories of human occurrence given the multitudes of lives that have occupied this world. The purpose for human life, human awareness eludes constricted conceptualization.

Etchings are more survivable than digital media yet limited by the conditions of that recording media. More effective communication historically has been more fragile. Accumulations of knowledge and power increase the likelihood of contention succeeding to erasure. Discoveries and improvements historically were mingled with objectionable cultures, philosophies and religions that invited destruction. Lacking a generally accepted carrier, a granite inscription standard, or a codex and scroll international repository history does not survive dissolution or destruction of societies. Without an accepted medium to attract and preserve accounts of events, history succumbs to random evaporation or purposeful destruction. Histories of human accumulation, archeological discoveries or studies of human genetics are incomplete. Indisputable proof of a creator or for evolution does not exist. The meaning of/for human life, human awareness is choice.

Gen 11:4 And they said, Go to, let us build us a city and a tower, whose top [may reach] unto heaven; and let us make us a name, lest we be scattered abroad upon the face of the whole earth.

Humans are infants, children, and then preadolescent before adulthood much like knowledge among evolving beings and cultures would develop. Early in societal development, without direction from a mentoring influence, barbarism, murder, paganism and war could be considered vestiges of pre evolved survival yet how do evolutionarily refined beings regress into warfare? At what stage does destructive behavior cease, or is intelligence subordinated to the physical environment? The physical environment is the creator in the evolutionary model.

Certainly a coalescing of intelligence would display fits and starts before societies got recording history right but what about created humans? Conveying events through symbols seems not to have been one of the first priorities. Possibly oral tradition may have been reliable before treachery motivated a desire to preserve accounts of events apart from agents of distortion. After all, the human family should have enjoyed a sense of sibling respect and trust but murder is ultimate denial; a severing of all entwined with the life taken. Maybe early humans were too strong and certain to be concerned for the direction of God. Created humans might have been appalled at being wrenched into a foreign reality and too stunned or ashamed to commit their account to others. Their minds were torn and expelled from their life spring.

Exd 23:1 Thou shalt not raise a false report: put not thine hand with the wicked to be an unrighteous witness.

16

Adam and Eve would have been shocked, challenged to manage the loss of bliss. The Garden of Eden was verdant, pristine creation. It is cited among other magnificences used to describe the glory of Lucifer.

Eze 28:13 Thou hast been in Eden the garden of God; every precious stone [was] thy covering, the sardius, topaz, and the diamond, the beryl, the onyx, and the jasper, the sapphire, the emerald, and the carbuncle, and gold: the workmanship of thy tabrets and of thy pipes was prepared in thee in the day that thou wast created.
Gen 3:6 And when the woman saw that the tree [was] good for food, and that it [was] pleasant to the eyes, and a tree to be desired to make [one] wise, she took of the fruit thereof, and did eat, and gave also unto her husband with her; and he did eat.
Gen 3:24 So he drove out the man; and he placed at the east of the garden of Eden Cherubims, and a flaming sword which turned every way, to keep the way of the tree of life.

We who biblically are 60 centuries removed may only begin to imagine the pain, regret and loss. Our minds are full of centuries of accumulated experience. How would first time minds encounter a new, a raw world? Did the knowledge of good and evil, the first time cares and concerns of this world persist to redirect and command their attention?

Gen 4:2 And she again bare his brother Abel. And Abel was a keeper of sheep, but Cain was a tiller of the ground.
Gen 4:3 And in process of time it came to pass, that Cain brought of the fruit of the ground an offering unto the LORD.

Gen 4:4 And Abel, he also brought of the firstlings of his flock and of the fat thereof. And the LORD had respect unto Abel and to his offering:
Gen 4:5 But unto Cain and to his offering he had not respect. And Cain was very wroth, and his countenance fell.
Gen 4:16 And Cain went out from the presence of the LORD, and dwelt in the land of Nod, on the east of Eden.
Gen 4:17 And Cain knew his wife; and she conceived, and bare Enoch: and he builded a city, and called the name of the city, after the name of his son, Enoch.

Did a worldwide flood erase the very evidence of human history except for massive stone works? Beings living over 800 years would have been powerful. Those long lives would "be history" without our need for written records. What conventions and cultures would arise from accumulations of physically superb people? To resolve their curiosity of the beginning some search for the first biblical site. Idyllic conditions necessarily include peaceful habitation. Through the contention of disobedience Adam and Eve were bereft of God, lost their standing and the garden life ended. Eden was larger than the Garden.

Gen 2:8 And the LORD God planted a garden eastward in Eden; and there he put the man whom he had formed.
Gen 2:10 And a river went out of Eden to water the garden; and from thence it was parted, and became into four heads.

Searching to ascertain "human", reconcile being and for our causal origin led science to postulate the initial mechanism for life. A creator free generation of life is posited to have necessarily begun at a very simple occurrence that increased in complexity through the appearance of new characteristics suitable for the physical conditions of existence. The choice for the first occurrence of life has defaulted to the single cell origin concept since physical evidence of the spontaneous appearance of complex life forms does not exist and cannot be created by any human science.   Here too there is no known capability to construct and animate the simple cell to prove this possibility. Evolution proposes the impersonal progression of natural selection for our existence.

Faith is the easy choice for anyone that requires nothing but to believe. The simple and sophisticated are all availed of the same reasoning and hope. This has generated the critical opinion that instance can occur where some who are either uneducated, malleable or without culled proficiency for guidance are prone to be manipulated and are of the type responsible for much of historical mayhem. The bible contains references to angels and insists for spiritual attainment. Incredible assertions ascribed to faith and spirit throughout scripture are disdained by modern persons who trust more in the sophistication of science and find no evidence of this spiritual life.

2Pe 3:16 As also in all [his] epistles, speaking in them of these things; in which are some things hard to be understood, which they that are unlearned and unstable wrest, as [they do] also the other scriptures, unto their own destruction.

Sin as the cause of all manner of cruel behavior is another side of the creation/evolution controversy. Here the point of contention between biblical revelation and evolution is evident. Evolved humans are considered to be progressing on toward perfection. Biblical revelation proposes:

Gen 6:5 And GOD saw that the wickedness of man [was] great in the earth, and [that] every imagination of the thoughts of his heart [was] only evil continually. Jer 17:9 The heart [is] deceitful above all [things], and desperately wicked: who can know it?

Rom 6:23 For the wages of sin [is] death; but the gift of God [is] eternal life through Jesus Christ our Lord.

The physical world is a place of trial, the proving ground of will. Religions and traditions of populations throughout the earth have elements that support either evolution or biblical revelation obliquely. This condition can be expected as dispersion followed from the point of origin. Who and what we are is drastically different than evolved happenings according to God's account. Biblically the human story commences with Adam and Eve's genesis, their fall and generation of children in their likeness. Humanity then exists as a consequence of either the biblical version or surmised evolution for the purposes of this study. Is the source of humanity a creator with purpose or an impersonal occurrence through suitability for physical conditions espoused by evolutionists? Did human awareness, our consciousness incidentally coalesce after adaptation through millions of ages? As we tread on our ancestors our question should be, shall we wait for several thousands of years to possibly evolve further? Are human faculties to remain idle while abiding evolution or is it time to seriously consider biblical revelation? The logical next step for evolutionists is to consciously alter humans by applying the capabilities that have developed up to this moment. Now evolution may transcend the natural selection process to exercise the function of creation, choice.

Choice is incumbent of separate physical entities. Awareness governs the potential significance of choice. Choice for individuals accountable to a greater entity is tempered as circumscribed by the greater entity. Life that arrives from a confluence of conditions is accountable to nothing. The source of human life is the license to human conduct. Human being, the perceptions, evaluation, intentions and conception of self align with ancients and will continue with our descendants. We do not know more than the rest; we are to choose. Creation is choice, volition, responsibility. Evolution occurs.

Guidance for Fateful Decisions

There are several reasons why we are ambivalent about "who and what we are". Science is certain of times and events through discoveries, geological assessments and application of scientific disciplines verified by critical review of proofs in journals and other venues. Authority seems to be somewhat less candid that the missing elements in the theory of evolution actually render it insufficient to withstand evaluation of the data. Rehearsing a faulty concept over several generations secures acceptance yet unexamined recognition does not amend the error. Evolution is aptly noted as theory. It is incongruous to mandate one theory to the exclusion of others if we truly seek to discover who we are. Theories of substance will rise and fall yet also deliver us closer to understanding who we are in the process. It is notable that natural selection does not hold out much promise for those who require a helping hand or the meek. The contest to attain acknowledgement of one theory over another however, is prone to cull vestiges of the contradicting opponent. Truce is not tolerated when contesting for the power of compulsion. Survival of the fittest is most discomforting in uncertain times unless one is at the very top of their capabilities and on the prevailing side.

Biblical ministries involve mercy, forgiveness, grace, redemption, a new life and ultimately returning to God. The fervent intentions of ministries however, struggle to get past the individual who am I. Solutions presented in parts do not have the strength of those same concepts committed to fulfilling an accepted purpose. The cornucopia of denominations does appear to desiccate the expected fruit. The divided message is an additional impediment for those who work to impart the biblical revelation of who and what we are to a skeptical audience. Churches are storehouses and indeed places of worship. The comfort and support of these places, exclusiveness and too much religion however divert the testimony of Christian sects. Christians are discomforted with the inherent message of their creator. They are stalled in solace and comfort. Commonly Christians commit less than the whole effort necessary to share the gospel of salvation lest they offend. There is finality to opportunity. A quiet example and loving spirit must eventually hazard the fire to preach the treasure of God.

Act 13:38 Be it known unto you therefore, men [and] brethren, that through this man is preached unto you the forgiveness of sins:
Act 13:39 And by him all that believe are justified from all things, from which ye could not be justified by the law of Moses.
Act 13:40 Beware therefore, lest that come upon you, which is spoken of in the prophets;
Act 13:41 Behold, ye despisers, and wonder, and perish: for I work a work in your days, a work which ye shall in no wise believe, though a man declare it unto you.
Jhn 3:7 Marvel not that I said unto thee, Ye must be born again.

The biblical message of who and what we are is contested by those who assert that evolution is the actual course of human genesis. Evolution arose from human investigation and the application of science.   Naturally theory that delivered the mechanical, medical and digital advances freeing present societies from subsistence living and disease is the preferred approach for professionals within these disciplines and also those who are comforted through such innovation. Since evolution developed from and continues to be adjusted by these same human disciplines it conforms to human concepts and thinking. People are inclined to choose that which is comfortable, that which makes sense.

Biblical revelation contains assertions that cannot be proven by science. Revelation delivers concepts that are discomforting and must be accepted by faith. In this regard those who believe in a creator assert that proofs for evolution do not sufficiently describe human being and so acknowledge a disconnection between the theory and realities of awareness, presence, purpose and spirit. While much can be learned through investigation of the benefit of biblical principles for societies science rather prefers its own creation. The bible is entwined with history and often is associated with the struggles of the past rather than for the guidance that eventually proved human dignity thereby liberating us from deprivation, manipulation and cruelty suffered by the majority of human populations historically and yet today. Religion has also been a cruel yoke of its own through the ages exercising purposes apart from the salvation message. Biblical efficacy is evidenced in governing documents of free peoples. The United States Declaration of Independence is predicated on biblical concepts as noted in the statement, "We hold these truths to be self-evident, that all men are created equal, that they are endowed by their Creator with certain unalienable rights." All, not only citizens but every person is innately worthy. Contrary to human behavior the Bible insists that we are all brothers and sisters in the image of God.

1Jo 3:11 For this is the message that ye heard from the beginning, that we should love one another.
1Jo 3:12 Not as Cain, [who] was of that wicked one, and slew his brother. And wherefore slew he him? Because his own works were evil, and his brother's righteous.
1Jo 3:14 We know that we have passed from death unto life, because we love the brethren. He that loveth not [his] brother abideth in death.
1Jo 3:15 Whosoever hateth his brother is a murderer: and ye know that no murderer hath eternal life abiding in him.
Mat 5:43 Ye have heard that it hath been said, Thou shalt love thy neighbour, and hate thine enemy.
Mat 5:44 But I say unto you, Love your enemies, bless them that curse you, do good to them that hate you,

and pray for them which despitefully use you, and persecute you;

Mat 5:45 That ye may be the children of your Father which is in heaven: for he maketh his sun to rise on the evil and on the good, and sendeth rain on the just and on the unjust.

Mat 5:46 For if ye love them which love you, what reward have ye? do not even the publicans the same?

Mat 5:47 And if ye salute your brethren only, what do ye more [than others]? do not even the publicans so?

Mat 5:48 Be ye therefore perfect, even as your Father which is in heaven is perfect.

Luk 6:35 But love ye your enemies, and do good, and lend, hoping for nothing again; and your reward shall be great, and ye shall be the children of the Highest: for he is kind unto the unthankful and [to] the evil.

1Jo 4:12 No man hath seen God at any time. If we love one another, God dwelleth in us, and his love is perfected in us.

1Jo 4:16 And we have known and believed the love that God hath to us. God is love; and he that dwelleth in love dwelleth in God, and God in him.

1Jo 4:21 And this commandment have we from him, That he who loveth God love his brother also.

Jhn 13:34 A new commandment I give unto you, That ye love one another; as I have loved you, that ye also love one another.

Jhn 15:12 This is my commandment, That ye love one another, as I have loved you.

Jhn 15:17 These things I command you, that ye love one another.

1Th 4:9 But as touching brotherly love ye need not that I write unto you: for ye yourselves are taught of God to love one another.

1Jo 4:7 Beloved, let us love one another: for love is of God; and every one that loveth is born of God, and knoweth God.

Scripture discomforts our beliefs and the accustomed manner of life. Revelation is delivery of concepts that do not arise from the natural world that we inhabit. Our true origin is unverifiable with current human knowledge. The immense influence the bible has exerted throughout human experience induced many attempts to determine the actual source or fable that produced the scriptures rendering nearly as many explanations. The bible could be the expressed mentality of human thought arising from those immersed in matters of this nature. The bible survives languages, nations and histories which have felled other human philosophies. Human thought then does not produce such lasting concepts providing evidence that this is not a source of the exclusive tome that is the bible. This book seeks to know the literal purpose expressed through the bible apart from investigations of who, what or where to prove or disprove but rather this search attempts to obtain the superhuman perspective. There must be then, elements of biblical scriptures that are contrary to human practice and tendencies. This condition is revelation. The bible declares that God has inspired and effected directions for human behavior in continuance of His creation purpose and process.

Gen 5:1 This [is] the book of the generations of Adam. In the day that God created man, in the likeness of God made He him;
Gen 5:2 Male and female created He them; and blessed them, and called their name Adam, in the day when they were created.
1Cr 15:45 And so it is written, The first man Adam was made a living soul; the last Adam [was made] a quickening spirit.
1Cr 15:47 The first man [is] of the earth, earthy: the second man [is] the Lord from heaven.
Isa 55:8 For my thoughts [are] not your thoughts, neither [are] your ways my ways, saith the LORD.
Isa 55:11 So shall my word be that goeth forth out of my mouth: it shall not return unto me void, but it shall

accomplish that which I please, and it shall prosper [in the thing] whereto I sent it.

Challenge can be an opportunity of contrast and an inducement to examine biblical revelation. It naturally follows then to consider creation from the first through the last chapter of the bible that is the account of human creation. Biblically the revelation of human being has been pre-recorded. Beings outside of time view the whole panorama of human existence.

Whether historical events are simply missing from human renditions or have been scrambled or forgotten for peace of conscience the absence of facts abets the theory of evolution. The sense of random order and apparent simplicity of the Genesis version is often discounted as ancient and indistinct, more figurative than literal and likely passed over for clearer passages of scripture. This conception disdains the revelation comprising the bible. The biblical account is either imagined or truly is the record of humanity beginning at the Garden. Could the uncomfortable arrangement of the first chapters of Genesis reveal a transition from spiritual to physical perception? How do those outside of time perceive and express events? Days are left behind by those who leave this planet or only recognized for human affairs by the deathless. The bible is either the will and word of God or it is no more than a culture's mysticism and philosophy fit only for understanding the motivation for a peoples' course in history. To the contrary, the preponderance of biblical revelation alters philosophies and life perspectives challenging even ardent unbelief.

Creation is Choice

Gen 1:26 And God said, Let us make man in our image, after our likeness: and let them have dominion over the fish of the sea, and over the fowl of the air, and over the cattle, and over all the earth, and over every creeping thing that creepeth upon the earth.

Gen 3:4 And the serpent said unto the woman, Ye shall not surely die:
Gen 3:5 For God doth know that in the day ye eat thereof, then your eyes shall be opened, and ye shall be as gods, knowing good and evil.
Gen 3:6 And when the woman saw that the tree [was] good for food, and that it [was] pleasant to the eyes, and a tree to be desired to make [one] wise, she took of the fruit thereof, and did eat, and gave also unto her husband with her; and he did eat.
Jam 1:15 Then when lust hath conceived, it bringeth forth sin: and sin, when it is finished, bringeth forth death.

From this Genesis event, when humans chose apart from God's will and severed His Holy Spirit, all biblical scriptures relate and sequentially reveal God's solution that is in fact underway. God's toleration of evil, iniquity and rebellion contradicts humanity's practice to establish and defend societies which is of great discomfort for unbelievers. The book of Genesis reveals humanity's condition without God. There is more to wisdom than people credit. God will not interfere with personal choice because it is a gift, "for the gifts and calling of God are without repentance." Choice is the most precious ability for individuals. Choice is the person; it confirms, expresses their presence, their existence. There is no purpose for judgment without choice. How could evolution/evolutionists be judged when elimination of the incapable is the engine of creation in this theory?

Rom 11:29 For the gifts and calling of God [are] without repentance.
Mat 25:31 When the Son of man shall come in his glory, and all the holy angels with him, then shall he sit upon the throne of his glory:
Mat 25:32 And before him shall be gathered all nations: and he shall separate them one from another, as a shepherd divideth [his] sheep from the goats:

27

Mat 25:33 And he shall set the sheep on his right hand, but the goats on the left.
Mat 25:34 Then shall the King say unto them on his right hand, Come, ye blessed of my Father, inherit the kingdom prepared for you from the foundation of the world:
Rev 20:12 And I saw the dead, small and great, stand before God; and the books were opened: and another book was opened, which is [the book] of life: and the dead were judged out of those things which were written in the books, according to their works.
Rev 20:13 And the sea gave up the dead which were in it; and death and hell delivered up the dead which were in them: and they were judged every man according to their works.
Rev 20:14 And death and hell were cast into the lake of fire. This is the second death.
Rev 20:15 And whosoever was not found written in the book of life was cast into the lake of fire.

Evolution theory asserts that life assembles from universal elements conforming to the conditions that occur on this planet not by an entity who, or that creates. Immutable natural law caused this universe at the big bang according to cosmology science. This science has publicly announced that God does not exist thereby freeing humanity from biblical constraints to enter the new age of discovery. These same irresistible forces and evolution theory portend humanity will soon arrive at a mass reduction as we expand beyond the sustainable population capacity of this planet. Human populations consume ages of accumulated resources generated by these optimum planetary conditions in a brief historical moment. Evolution damages humanity by diminishing the functions of choice since natural selection occurs without conscious direction. The mindless progression of cosmic forces and evolution theory are incongruent with human behavior, with human being echoing a willful creator. As God is expunged the human species will learn which explanation accurately portrays human motivation, history and attainment or conclusion. The apple still dangling out of reach will deliver the reason for us, happenstance or purpose. God however has not abandoned us to sin, reduction and death. Adam and Eve were warned. The children of God choose Him. All the rest choose to contradict the Creator of life.

Gal 4:3 Even so we, when we were children, were in bondage under the elements of the world:
Gal 4:4 But when the fulness of the time was come, God sent forth his Son, made of a woman, made under the law,
Gal 4:5 To redeem them that were under the law, that we might receive the adoption of sons.
Gal 4:6 And because ye are sons, God hath sent forth the Spirit of his Son into your hearts, crying, Abba, Father.
Gal 4:7 Wherefore thou art no more a servant, but a son; and if a son, then an heir of God through Christ.

Jhn 3:16 For God so loved the world, that he gave his only begotten Son, that whosoever believeth in him should not perish, but have everlasting life.

1Cr 2:7 But we speak the wisdom of God in a mystery, [even] the hidden [wisdom], which God ordained before the world unto our glory:
1Cr 2:8 Which none of the princes of this world knew: for had they known [it], they would not have crucified the Lord of glory.
1Cr 2:9 But as it is written, Eye hath not seen, nor ear heard, neither have entered into the heart of man, the things which God hath prepared for them that love him.
1Cr 2:10 But God hath revealed [them] unto us by his Spirit: for the Spirit searcheth all things, yea, the deep things of God.

Chapter 2
Your Adversary

A Bloodthirsty Thorn in Eden,

Eze 28:13 Thou hast been in Eden the garden of God; every precious stone [was] thy covering, the sardius, topaz, and the diamond, the beryl, the onyx, and the jasper, the sapphire, the emerald, and the carbuncle, and gold: the workmanship of thy tabrets and of thy pipes was prepared in thee in the day that thou wast created.
Eze 28:14 Thou [art] the anointed cherub that covereth; and I have set thee [so]: thou wast upon the holy mountain of God; thou hast walked up and down in the midst of the stones of fire.
Eze 28:15 Thou [wast] perfect in thy ways from the day that thou wast created, till iniquity was found in thee.
Eze 28:16 By the multitude of thy merchandise they have filled the midst of thee with violence, and thou hast sinned: therefore I will cast thee as profane out of the mountain of God: and I will destroy thee, O covering cherub, from the midst of the stones of fire.
Isa 14:12 How art thou fallen from heaven, O Lucifer, son of the morning! [how] art thou cut down to the ground, which didst weaken the nations!
Isa 14:13 For thou hast said in thine heart, I will ascend into heaven, I will exalt my throne above the stars of God: I will sit also upon the mount of the congregation, in the sides of the north:
Isa 14:14 I will ascend above the heights of the clouds; I will be like the most High.
Isa 14:15 Yet thou shalt be brought down to hell, to the sides of the pit.

This being is the original perpetrator of opposition who is identified by many names that describe his purpose where he is noted in scripture. Lucifer depicts illumination, the shining one or bright star. Every precious stone was his covering who was created the anointed cherub and son of the morning. He was truly a light and a focal point for beauty. His own heart however was alien to the created position; prideful, he is offensive and profane. Lucifer willfully exercised an image of opposition who was filled with contention so assured it eventually falls to violence. Through his choices he changed into a different entity than the creator's will, the anointed cherub. He became gross, degraded into the angel of darkness who continually conformed to darkness rather than light. Eventually as the name indicates his choices led him to become Satan, the standard of exclusive self, pride and engrossed with personal attainment. Choices of this kind will align with Satan's image. Our lives are not solitary.

Jam 3:16 For where envying and strife [is], there [is] confusion and every evil work.
Jhn 8:44 Ye are of [your] father the devil, and the lusts of your father ye will do. He was a murderer from the beginning, and abode not in the truth, because there is no truth in him. When he speaketh a lie, he speaketh of his own: for he is a liar, and the father of it.

Multitude of Your Merchandise

Consider the sparkling description of Lucifer and yet the bible does not state that he was created in the image of God. This wondrous being could not allow a species in the image of God to exceed his presence. The serpent personifies this truth through his determination to debase, misdirect and otherwise corrupt human kind. Pre event information within biblical scripture that would allow us to understand more of the temptation in the Garden is scant regarding the serpent. However the strange arrangement of roles in the garden experience is stark convention to express that which is in play. Jealousy does not heed limitations for the being entirely focused on self. The behavior of the tempter before the temptation in the Garden is not noted, he simply appears. Adam and Eve were unaware of the serpent's consuming passion. The serpent contradicts God. Without preliminary circumstance the subtle serpent suggests God is the deceiver Who prevents full human attainment. Discussion with a serpent does not seem uncommon to the woman; it is the subject itself that is grossly rapine in the depravity of the question amidst the wonder of creation. Biblical scripture only recognizes the manifestation of this behavior as a multitude of merchandise that filled the serpent, the Devil, Satan with violence and declares that he has sinned. We do not know when the Original Sin occurred but the originator is known when sin is passed from Satan to humans at the garden temptation. Rejection, rebellion, contempt and offense came into being in Satan. Lucifer was in Eden, was cast out of the mountain of God and destroyed from the midst of fiery stones at times undefined because events are more significant than time to immortals. Lucifer might have been in transition at the Garden temptation but certainly transformed then if not before into the Devil or Satan in rebellion. The "great red dragon", "that old serpent", "the accuser of the brethren", was cast out into the earth later in the 12th chapter of Revelation after "a man child who was to rule all nations with a rod of iron", was "caught up to God and to His throne".

Gen 3:1 Now the serpent was more subtil than any beast of the field which the LORD God had made. And he said unto the woman, Yea, hath God said, Ye shall not eat of every tree of the garden?
Gen 3:2 And the woman said unto the serpent, We may eat of the fruit of the trees of the garden:
Gen 3:3 But of the fruit of the tree which [is] in the midst of the garden, God hath said, Ye shall not eat of it, neither shall ye touch it, lest ye die.
Gen 3:4 And the serpent said unto the woman, Ye shall not surely die:

Gen 3:5 For God doth know that in the day ye eat thereof, then your eyes shall be opened, and ye shall be as gods, knowing good and evil.

Rev 12:5 And she brought forth a man child, who was to rule all nations with a rod of iron: and her child was caught up unto God, and [to] his throne.

Rev 12:7 And there was war in heaven: Michael and his angels fought against the dragon; and the dragon fought and his angels,

Rev 12:8 And prevailed not; neither was their place found any more in heaven.

Rev 12:9 And the great dragon was cast out, that old serpent, called the Devil, and Satan, which deceiveth the whole world: he was cast out into the earth, and his angels were cast out with him.

The Garden temptation was part of the accumulation "multitude of your merchandise" that proved and eventually evicted the profane serpent, the devil, Satan from the mountain of God. A multitude of merchandise does appear to speak of more than one event and indicates tolerance or forgiveness that expects or at least leaves room for repentance. Comportment, events and summation names are accounted by the deathless who have no concern for time. We do not change names as God does. God speaks the name of each being's manifestation, what they are. Changing names is not common in this world. Some change their name to conceal their identity; others take a different name to avoid hindrances while interacting within a foreign culture. Titles are appended to names and marriage arranges names in recognition of the union. Our names identify with an ancestor, family or culture rather than our own manifestation. We do not choose to come into existence and are not involved in our first name. First naming is set to specific roles in Genesis. God presented animals to Adam to see what he would name them. Naming is a revelation of the namer and additionally enables spirit to know more of the physical/spirit perception of existence. Names may not develop for life that occurs apart from choice.

Gen 2:19 And out of the ground the LORD God formed every beast of the field, and every fowl of the air; and brought [them] unto Adam to see what he would call them: and whatsoever Adam called every living creature, that [was] the name thereof.
Gen 2:20 And Adam gave names to all cattle, and to the fowl of the air, and to every beast of the field; but for Adam there was not found an help meet for him.
Gen 17:5 Neither shall thy name any more be called Abram, but thy name shall be Abraham; for a father of many nations have I made thee.
Gen 17:15 And God said unto Abraham, As for Sarai thy wife, thou shalt not call her name Sarai, but Sarah [shall] her name [be].
Mar 8:33 But when he had turned about and looked on his disciples, he rebuked Peter, saying, Get thee behind me, Satan: for thou savourest not the things that be of God, but the things that be of men.
Jhn 1:42 And he brought him to Jesus. And when Jesus beheld him, he said, Thou art Simon the son of Jona: thou shalt be called Cephas, which is by interpretation, a stone.

A different description is used for the Garden tempter, of the same species as a dragon, yet the lowly state of this tempter allows stealth and deception. The tempter may have merely been driven to act from jealousy that had prevailed over sanity. Thoughtless reaction to an opponent is not indicated in this account however. The tempter does not exhibit any evidence of caution to manage the displeasure of God for despoiling His creation. The tempter disdains the Spirit of God. The cunning involved indicates more than a desire to eliminate or otherwise ruin humans. The devil, Satan's actions and words reveal a being who esteems himself a fellow, at least an equal with God. This account evidences a contest where the tempter has decided to woo and take over all creation. A dragon is the epitome, awesome and grand compared to a serpent.

Cunning Serpent

Motive focuses the understanding of who we are. Who we are could simply be one more casualty of the struggle between good and evil. If Adam and Eve were as wildlife unhomed by loggers they would need no more identity than to be mentioned as humans. A cunning serpent is then overkill and a senseless extravagance. What is the significance of tempting Eve? Was it harder to attempt the first created than the second? It is rather, more opportunistic to affect the human component with the greatest influence over new life from this point forward from creation. Additionally, placing a contention between the two elements of human existence is a very effective strategy for destruction. The tempter applied all subtlety to entice Eve and then carry Adam. We continue to be "beguiled" still today.

2Cr 11:3 But I fear, lest by any means, as the serpent beguiled Eve through his subtilty, so your minds should be corrupted from the simplicity that is in Christ.

Cunning does betray motive. Adam and Eve were more than an experiment of curiosity on an obscure world. Their creation in the image of God, the One Who is the center of all could not be hidden or secret. The garden of God adds more celebrity to these new creatures. Created in the image of the Supreme Being and placed in His garden Adam and Eve were among the jewels of God's glory. This glory was grossly, obscenely interrupted. Creation is the performance of God's anticipation. Human accomplishment is now inhibited chrysalis like to discover those hearts that align with the human being God is creating. We do not esteem our real purpose but utmost through the entirety of human being is the word of God. God is creating humans in His image. There will be human beings in the image of God to His glory.

Isa 55:11 So shall my word be that goeth forth out of my mouth: it shall not return unto me void, but it shall accomplish that which I please, and it shall prosper [in the thing] whereto I sent it.
Rev 1:2 Who bare record of the word of God, and of the testimony of Jesus Christ, and of all things that he saw.
Rev 19:10 And I fell at his feet to worship him. And he said unto me, See [thou do it] not: I am thy fellowservant, and of thy brethren that have the testimony of Jesus: worship God: for the testimony of Jesus is the spirit of prophecy.

Gen 2:25 And they were both naked, the man and his wife, and were not ashamed.

Adam and Eve were open, the objects of rapt attention, yet unmindful of their stature. They were naked, exposed to matters of creative, elemental initiatives yet unburdened with their gravity. "The man", does not have a name until Genesis 2:19 where he is now "Adam". Adam does have a name before the temptation but the woman has no name until after the temptation, fall and pronouncements. Eve is "the woman" in eleven instances until she is named in Genesis 3:20 and then only once again at verse 4:1 is she called Eve in Genesis. It was not about who they were before they chose apart from the will of God. It seems they became more aware of themselves, the individual who, with their fall.

Creation here departs from the course that God would have preferred. The omniscience of those in the image of God was lost to human being. Those concerned with who, the individual self have limited percipience and are prone to arrive at faulty conclusions such as pride and thereby are open to all manner of ungodliness. Our focus is misdirected. We are now distracted and deceived, caught up with whom and languishing in the web of deceit cast over our understanding. The restriction of our awareness renders us more susceptible to our desires and the deceptions and schemes of the silken and glib tongued archfiend. Our understanding is still "naked"; we continue the display, we are still on stage. Our audience is the deathless. Human being will be exquisite jewels of God's glory when our aspect of His creation is fulfilled.

2Cr 11:13 For such [are] false apostles, deceitful workers, transforming themselves into the apostles of Christ.
2Cr 11:14 And no marvel; for Satan himself is transformed into an angel of light.
2Cr 11:15 Therefore [it is] no great thing if his ministers also be transformed as the ministers of righteousness; whose end shall be according to their works.
1Pe 1:12 Unto whom it was revealed, that not unto themselves, but unto us they did minister the things, which are now reported unto you by them that have preached the gospel unto you with the Holy Ghost sent down from heaven; which things the angels desire to look into.

The pre tempter was truly a wondrous being. He was glorious in all his ways, the covering cherub and the son of the morning. Our understanding fails with the incomprehensible majesty of God's anointed cherub yet he was created a beautiful being. Satan's will, his own mind of creation corrupted himself being wholly captive in self esteem. Satan chooses to oppose God. Though approaching Eve in a lesser form he was confident that he was at least God's equal. Why tempt the man and woman? His mindset is clear as he says when tempting Eve." ye shall be as gods ".

Gen 3:5 For God doth know that in the day ye eat thereof, then your eyes shall be opened, and ye shall be as gods, knowing good and evil.
Isa 14:13 For thou hast said in thine heart, I will ascend into heaven, I will exalt my throne above the stars of God: I will sit also upon the mount of the congregation, in the sides of the north:
Isa 14:14 I will ascend above the heights of the clouds; I will be like the most High.
Mat 4:8 Again, the devil taketh him up into an exceeding high mountain, and sheweth him all the kingdoms of the world, and the glory of them;
Mat 4:9 And saith unto him, All these things will I give thee, if thou wilt fall down and worship me.

Satan, the angels and humans are not able to know the purposes of God except that which He chooses to reveal to us. The devil quotes scripture while tempting Jesus.

1Jo 4:1 Beloved, believe not every spirit, but try the spirits whether they are of God: because many false prophets are gone out into the world.
Mat 24:36 But of that day and hour knoweth no [man], no, not the angels of heaven, but my Father only.
Mat 4:6 And saith unto him, If thou be the Son of God, cast thyself down: for it is written, He shall give his angels charge concerning thee: and in [their] hands they shall bear thee up, lest at any time thou dash thy foot against a stone.
Psa 91:11 For he shall give his angels charge over thee, to keep thee in all thy ways.
2Pe 1:21 For the prophecy came not in old time by the will of man: but holy men of God spake [as they were] moved by the Holy Ghost.

How absolutely vain or wholly ruinous is Satan to persist despite pronouncements of his eventual defeat. The extents for evil and destruction have not yet been fully plumbed by this mighty being who discounts statements of his demise. The creation of humans was not concluded in the garden. The contention over our very existence is witness that expects fulfillment. We are not aware that the conduct of our lives, our living is participating in this warfare. Our lives, our concepts of reality, our purposes conform to the specific location and culture of our occupation. Worldwide communications are reordering this historical condition into a collective consciousness. Individuals look for a kind of marketplace of commerce that enhances the lives of all. Ideally in a collection of philosophies the most worthwhile succeeds. This expectation and hope relies on behaviors that do not comport with history. The influence of interaction among individuals is subsumed in a multitude. Governance accountable to individual influence conforms to the requirements and expectations of the governed. Governance insulated from judgment exercises compulsion and is the bane of the governed. The products of knowledge are affecting worldwide alignments that now are more conformable to biblical end time descriptions which were hard to place in previous world orders. Humans require the tree of life to live forever but spirits are not so constrained. Satan's fate was revealed two thousand years ago to us and so thereby to all spirits. Satan disputes the Word of God.

Luk 4:7 If thou therefore wilt worship me, all shall be thine.
Luk 4:8 and Jesus answered and said unto him, Get thee behind me, Satan: for it is written, Thou shalt worship the Lord thy God, and him only shalt thou serve.
Jhn 10:10 The thief cometh not, but for to steal, and to kill, and to destroy: I am come that they might have life, and that they might have [it] more abundantly.

Jhn 12:31 Now is the judgment of this world: now shall the prince of this world be cast out.

Ultimate fulfillment for the self consumed mind is adulation. Complete human surrender and worship is pride's conquest and validation. The tempter's conditional, pre ascendant strategy determined to despoil, lessen or eliminate human beings created in the image of God. The created presumed to be greater than the creator with his intent to supplant God Himself. The conclusion challenges that creation is not exclusive to God. The irreverence and repudiation evidenced by the actions of the tempter elicit ominous expectations upon first considering this concept yet humanists seek similar achievements. Those who assert that evolving beings invented God during a pre-knowledge, primitive condition now seek to create life and to extend it. Experimental creation is a moral contradiction that portends woe until its logical conclusion. Government and creation suffer when wielded by the inadequate. History is the truth regarding human governments; they have all failed. This is the contest between creation and evolution the 2 acts of faith considered in this study. We have either been created by the physical world or God. We are creators of the structure of our lives, those who do not believe God and those who do. The proof of true creation is enduring, vibrant life. When God is involved the activity, contention or thoughts are absolute.

Gen 3:24 So He drove out the man; and He placed cherubim at the east of the Garden of Eden, and a flaming sword which turned every way, to guard the way to the tree of life.
Gen 6:5 and GOD saw that the wickedness of man [was] great in the earth, and [that] every imagination of the thoughts of his heart [was] only evil continually.
Gen 6:6 and it repented the LORD that he had made man on the earth, and it grieved him at his heart.
Gen 6:7 and the LORD said, I will destroy man whom I have created from the face of the earth; both man,

and beast, and the creeping thing, and the fowls of the air; for it repenteth me that I have made them.

Rev 12:1 And there appeared a great wonder in heaven; a woman clothed with the sun, and the moon under her feet, and upon her head a crown of twelve stars:
Rev 12:2 And she being with child cried, travailing in birth, and pained to be delivered.
Rev 12:3 And there appeared another wonder in heaven; and behold a great red dragon, having seven heads and ten horns, and seven crowns upon his heads.
Rev 12:4 And his tail drew the third part of the stars of heaven, and did cast them to the earth: and the dragon stood before the woman which was ready to be delivered, for to devour her child as soon as it was born.
Rev 12:5 And she brought forth a man child, who was to rule all nations with a rod of iron: and her child was caught up unto God, and [to] his throne.

Scriptural revelation of human conception and the disaster of the garden temptation seem utterly too fantastic to be believable for contemporary, sophisticated people but what Satan accomplished in the garden continues to resonate in biblical events and throughout the world. People perpetrate small and great wickedness on others. The genesis, our beginning and the challenge, the ignition of the contest of validity are truer renditions of the human condition and behavior than an evolution into human being. Ultimate confirmation awaits fulfillment of the prerecorded revelation of the human spectacle contained in the Judeo Christian Bible. The serpent was not exiled or confined apart where no further harm was possible but did not escape unscathed.

Gen 3:14 and the LORD God said unto the serpent, because thou hast done this, thou [art] cursed above

all cattle, and above every beast of the field; upon thy belly shalt thou go, and dust shalt thou eat all the days of thy life:
Gen 3:15 And I will put enmity between thee and the woman, and between thy seed and her seed; it shall bruise thy head, and thou shalt bruise his heel.

The contest is much more than jealous rivalry as Satan continues beyond pronouncements of his defeat. Satan does not seek reproachment with God. He sought to devour the Savior thereby preventing the redemption and salvation of humans. Having lost this chance he deceives the world to prevent salvation and still does not cease to accuse the brethren before the court of immortals presided over by God. Human being is the substance, the heart of the contention.

Rev 12:10 And I heard a loud voice saying in heaven, Now is come salvation, and strength, and the kingdom of our God, and the power of his Christ: for the accuser of our brethren is cast down, which accused them before our God day and night.

Incessant from the temptation of Adam and Eve humanity has remained the focus of a struggle, "that old serpent, called the Devil, and Satan, which deceiveth the whole world ". We presume too much early in our effort to navigate our lives. If we reconsider or recognize our place in creation is of such critical significance our striving would be more attuned to spiritual enlightenment, to seek whatever could be gleaned of who and what we are. Our thoughts might not be so completely consumed with the physical world around us. Our understanding has been confined in this current existence. Effort is necessary to extract oneself from the cares and concerns of this world if we seek to know who we are. Thought must have space from distraction. The essential pause, the peace required is necessarily extricated from the familiar. Each exercise of will in progression above the immediate demands of our surroundings is more difficult than the preceding effort.

1. Our presence and actions have immediate consequence in the physical world.
2. Planning and thought are more effective for our purposes although not immediately realized unlike our physical actions.
3. Spiritual concerns moreover require the suspension of physical desires while the benefit is less discernible early in the choice to seek the supernatural.

Skepticism of the spiritual follows from our experience, that which is common to us and is the physical condition of our existence. The spiritual world is alien to our present state. It will not arrive by sight, smell, sound, taste or touch. Spiritual concepts and perception transcend physical preoccupation. Human being is more than the physical world can provide, we are more than the animal. Who, what we are now is vastly more significant than has occurred to us anywhere our reasoning has wandered. Validity and truth are to be proven with the human display until the end of time when the mystery of God should be finished.

Rev 10:6 And sware by him that liveth for ever and ever, who created heaven, and the things that therein are, and the earth, and the things that therein are, and the sea, and the things which are therein, that there should be time no longer:
Rev 10:7but in the days of the voice of the seventh angel, when he shall begin to sound, the mystery of God should be finished, as he hath declared to his servants the prophets.

Mat 16:24 Then said Jesus unto his disciples, If any [man] will come after me, let him deny himself, and take up his cross, and follow me.
Mar 8:34 And when he had called the people [unto him] with his disciples also, he said unto them,

Whosoever will come after me, let him deny himself, and take up his cross, and follow me.

Luk 9:23 And he said to [them] all, If any [man] will come after me, let him deny himself, and take up his cross daily, and follow me.

2Pe 3:4 And saying, where is the promise of his coming? For since the fathers fell asleep, all things continue as [they were] from the beginning of the creation.

Consider this, all the effort, the purpose that is the bible points to the gravity of who and what we are, yet the physical world captures our attention. We are caught up with a deception. Naked is a rather stark word but not strong enough to bring us out of our somnolence. Naked describes who we are; subject to, "the prince of the power of the air, the spirit that now worketh in the children of disobedience:" We are indeed naked yet God urges us to awaken from the dead, shake off the deception and to dress.

Eph 2:1 and you [hath he quickened], who were dead in trespasses and sins;

Eph 2:2 wherein in time past ye walked according to the course of this world, according to the prince of the power of the air, the spirit that now worketh in the children of disobedience:

Eph 2:3 Among whom also we all had our conversation in times past in the lusts of our flesh, fulfilling the desires of the flesh and of the mind; and were by nature the children of wrath, even as others.

1Cr 13:12 For now we see through a glass, darkly; but then face to face: now I know in part; but then shall I know even as also I am known.

1Cr 4:11 Even unto this present hour we both hunger, and thirst, and are naked, and are buffeted, and have no certain dwellingplace;

2Cr 5:1 For we know that if our earthly house of [this] tabernacle were dissolved, we have a building of God, an house not made with hands, eternal in the heavens.

2Cr 5:2 for in this we groan, earnestly desiring to be clothed upon with our house which is from heaven:

2Cr 5:3 If so be that being clothed we shall not be found naked.

2Cr 5:4 For we that are in [this] tabernacle do groan, being burdened: not for that we would be unclothed, but clothed upon, that mortality might be swallowed up of life.

Eph 6:10 Finally, my brethren, be strong in the Lord, and in the power of his might.

Eph 6:11 Put on the whole armour of God, that ye may be able to stand against the wiles of the devil.

Eph 6:12 For we wrestle not against flesh and blood, but against principalities, against powers, against the rulers of the darkness of this world, against spiritual wickedness in high [places].

Eph 6:13 Wherefore take unto you the whole armour of God, that ye may be able to withstand in the evil day, and having done all, to stand.

The Wisdom of God

The wisdom of God suffers the power of rebellion thereby allowing human decision, human participation in creation. Decision does not merely damn or save the individual, it resonates throughout creation.

Rom 11:29 For the gifts and calling of God [are] without repentance.

Rom 11:33 O the depth of the riches both of the wisdom and knowledge of God! How unsearchable [are] his judgments, and his ways past finding out!

Rom 11:36 For of him, and through him, and to him, [are] all things: to whom [be] glory forever. Amen.

2Pe 2:1 But there were false prophets also among the people, even as there shall be false teachers among you, who privily shall bring in damnable heresies, even denying the Lord that bought them, and bring upon themselves swift destruction.
2Pe 2:2 And many shall follow their pernicious ways; by reason of whom the way of truth shall be evil spoken of.
2Pe 2:3 And through covetousness shall they with feigned words make merchandise of you: whose judgment now of a long time lingereth not, and their damnation slumbereth not.
Rev 12:9 And the great dragon was cast out, that old serpent, called the Devil, and Satan, which deceiveth the whole world: he was cast out into the earth, and his angels were cast out with him.

God succors us with lovingkindness, forgiveness, faithfulness, grace, patience and wisdom for all the human experience; in every, in all things to His glory. The existence, the purpose of human being is the controversy. Satan is accusatory, contemptuous, divisive and selfish. Satan has continued to assail humanity as can be seen in his description as the accuser of the brethren, "the accuser of our brethren is cast down, which accused them before our God day and night". The accusation is not leveled against an opponent. Satan is arguing the failure of this trifling thus contending that God is the inept creator. God allows iniquity and rebellion to their ruin and destruction or allows for proofs of creation. Truth will become known. We are given a lifetime to choose God. Those outside of time are witness.

Gen 4:7 If thou doest well, shalt thou not be accepted? And if thou doest not well, sin lieth at the door. And unto thee [shall be] his desire, and thou shalt rule over him.

46

Gen 15:16 But in the fourth generation they shall come hither again: for the iniquity of the Amorites [is] not yet full.
2Pe 3:15 and account [that] the longsuffering of our Lord [is] salvation; even as our beloved brother Paul also according to the wisdom given unto him hath written unto you;
1Cr 2:8 Which none of the princes of this world knew: for had they known [it], they would not have crucified the Lord of glory.

Satan's contention with God, gleaned from rather scant biblical glimpses for the breadth and duration of the opposition reveal a challenge of validity.   Actually, ignorance of the conflict prompts some to cite seemingly arbitrary disease and suffering for their rejection of the gospel message. However, human suffering did not exist in Eden.

Job 2:4 And Satan answered the LORD, and said, Skin for skin, yea, all that a man hath will he give for his life.
Job 2:5 But put forth thine hand now, and touch his bone and his flesh, and he will curse thee to thy face.

The matter is perplexing when considered in small instances but revelation is opened up by the human course in scripture. God directs and instructs. He is patient, merciful and faithful to sustain His children through to the fulfillment of His promise. Salvation is pending. Humans can be reunited with God, His Spirit, His promise to the completion, the recreation of human being. Creation is intended it does not simply occur. The choice to create must be acknowledged and confirmed by the choice to accept. The created accepts completing the circle to become and fulfill the Word of God.

Luk 24:49 And, behold, I send the promise of my Father upon you: but tarry ye in the city of Jerusalem, until ye be endued with power from on high.

Jhn 14:26 But the Comforter, [which is] the Holy Ghost, whom the Father will send in my name, he shall teach you all things, and bring all things to your remembrance, whatsoever I have said unto you.

Act 1:8 But ye shall receive power, after that the Holy Ghost is come upon you: and ye shall be witnesses unto me both in Jerusalem, and in all Judaea, and in Samaria, and unto the uttermost part of the earth.

Act 2:39 For the promise is unto you, and to your children, and to all that are afar off, [even] as many as the Lord our God shall call.

Rom 8:26 Likewise the Spirit also helpeth our infirmities: for we know not what we should pray for as we ought: but the Spirit itself maketh intercession for us with groanings which cannot be uttered.

Rom 8:27 And he that searcheth the hearts knoweth what [is] the mind of the Spirit, because he maketh intercession for the saints according to [the will of] God.

1Cr 2:12 Now we have received, not the spirit of the world, but the spirit which is of God; that we might know the things that are freely given to us of God.

1Cr 2:13 Which things also we speak, not in the words which man's wisdom teacheth, but which the Holy Ghost teacheth; comparing spiritual things with spiritual.

Eph 1:13 In whom ye also [trusted], after that ye heard the word of truth, the gospel of your salvation: in whom also after that ye believed, ye were sealed with that holy Spirit of promise,

Phl 1:28 And in nothing terrified by your adversaries: which is to them an evident token of perdition, but to you of salvation, and that of God.

Phl 2:12 Wherefore, my beloved, as ye have always obeyed, not as in my presence only, but now much more in my absence, work out your own salvation with fear and trembling.

1Pe 1:9 Receiving the end of your faith, [even] the salvation of [your] souls.

How tragic indeed are the ways of sinners. Sin is a blood thirsty thorn. The rebellion that has swept humans into the contest reveals a creation wide warfare.

Rev 12:6 And the woman fled into the wilderness, where she hath a place prepared of God, that they should feed her there a thousand two hundred [and] threescore days.
Rev 12:7 And there was war in heaven: Michael and his angels fought against the dragon; and the dragon fought and his angels,
Rev 12:8 And prevailed not; neither was their place found any more in heaven.
Rev 12:9 And the great dragon was cast out, that old serpent, called the Devil, and Satan, which deceiveth the whole world: he was cast out into the earth, and his angels were cast out with him.
Rev 12:10 And I heard a loud voice saying in heaven, Now is come salvation, and strength, and the kingdom of our God, and the power of his Christ: for the accuser of our brethren is cast down, which accused them before our God day and night.
Rev 12:11 And they overcame him by the blood of the Lamb, and by the word of their testimony; and they loved not their lives unto the death.

Witness

The act of God, the redemption through His blood, the sacrifice of the Lamb overcomes the testimony of the accuser as those who believe more assuredly than death verify their salvation and thereby disprove Satan's assertions. Humans in the image of God are now the witness. This is finally the victory of humans over the tempter, the archfiend, liar and wicked, evil murderer who committed to destroy us, our elemental enemy. The redemption, the work of God is finally fulfilled in the testimony of Jesus before the court of God to prove Satan is false. This proof expels Satan; seals his doom.

2Cr 5:21 For he hath made him [to be] sin for us, who knew no sin; that we might be made the righteousness of God in him.
Rev 12:12 therefore rejoice, [ye] heavens, and ye that dwell in them. Woe to the inhabiters of the earth and of the sea! for the devil is come down unto you, having great wrath, because he knoweth that he hath but a short time.
Rev 12:13 And when the dragon saw that he was cast unto the earth, he persecuted the woman which brought forth the man [child].
Rev 12:14 And to the woman were given two wings of a great eagle, that she might fly into the wilderness, into her place, where she is nourished for a time, and times, and half a time, from the face of the serpent.
Rev 12:15 And the serpent cast out of his mouth water as a flood after the woman, that he might cause her to be carried away of the flood.
Rev 12:16 And the earth helped the woman, and the earth opened her mouth, and swallowed up the flood which the dragon cast out of his mouth.
Rev 12:17 And the dragon was wroth with the woman, and went to make war with the remnant of her seed, which keep the commandments of God, and have the testimony of Jesus Christ.
Dan 7:19 Then I would know the truth of the fourth beast, which was diverse from all the others, exceeding dreadful, whose teeth [were of] iron, and his nails [of] brass; [which] devoured, brake in pieces, and stamped the residue with his feet;
Dan 7:20 And of the ten horns that [were] in his head, and [of] the other which came up, and before whom

three fell; even [of] that horn that had eyes, and a mouth that spake very great things, whose look [was] more stout than his fellows.

Dan 7:21 I beheld, and the same horn made war with the saints, and prevailed against them;

Dan 7:22 Until the Ancient of days came, and judgment was given to the saints of the most High; and the time came that the saints possessed the kingdom.

Dan 7:23 Thus he said, The fourth beast shall be the fourth kingdom upon earth, which shall be diverse from all kingdoms, and shall devour the whole earth, and shall tread it down, and break it in pieces.

Dan 7:24 And the ten horns out of this kingdom [are] ten kings [that] shall arise: and another shall rise after them; and he shall be diverse from the first, and he shall subdue three kings.

Dan 7:25 And he shall speak [great] words against the most High, and shall wear out the saints of the most High, and think to change times and laws: and they shall be given into his hand until a time and times and the dividing of time.

Dan 7:26 But the judgment shall sit, and they shall take away his dominion, to consume and to destroy [it] unto the end.

Dan 7:27 And the kingdom and dominion, and the greatness of the kingdom under the whole heaven, shall be given to the people of the saints of the most High, whose kingdom [is] an everlasting kingdom, and all dominions shall serve and obey him.

Dan 7:28 Hitherto [is] the end of the matter. As for me Daniel, my cogitations much troubled me, and my countenance changed in me: but I kept the matter in my heart.

Rev 20:2 and he laid hold on the dragon, that old serpent, which is the Devil, and Satan, and bound him a thousand years, and when the thousand years are expired, Satan shall be loosed out of his prison,

Rev 20:8 And shall go out to deceive the nations which are in the four quarters of the earth, Gog and Magog, to gather them together to battle: the number of whom [is] as the sand of the sea.

Rev 20:9 And they went up on the breadth of the earth, and compassed the camp of the saints about, and the beloved city: and fire came down from God out of heaven, and devoured them.

Rev 20:10 and the devil that deceived them was cast into the lake of fire and brimstone, where the beast and the false prophet [are], and shall be tormented day and night for ever and ever.

Chapter 3
Despoil or Utterly Ruin

Gen 1:26 And God said, Let us make man in our image, after our likeness: and let them have dominion over the fish of the sea, and over the fowl of the air, and over the cattle, and over all the earth, and over every creeping thing that creepeth upon the earth.

Awareness dismayed, scourged their being. In an instant Adam and Eve the image of God, full of His Spirit, lords over all the earth were bereft, torn from their Godness. Crushing shame drove them to hide. The potency of God, His Spirit and wisdom that enlightens, enlivens, invigorates to open understanding no longer dwelt in them. Our condition, our perception is incapable to comprehend the tragedy. The Creator of life succinctly depicted existence apart from His presence as death. God described the dire consequences of refuting His will in the unencumbered warning, "in the day that you eat thereof you shall surely die." The loss of the presence of the Creator is death where the debilitated now maneuver merely a physical presence. Suffering further effect thereof, after they ate the forbidden fruit and lost the Spirit of God, Adam and Eve were denied the tree of life. Humans without the Spirit of God stumble into afflictions, strife and reduction succeeding to death. We are physical, comparably speaking dead and subject to death.

Gen 2:17 But of the tree of the knowledge of good and evil, thou shalt not eat of it: for in the day that thou eatest thereof thou shalt surely die.
Gen 3:4 And the serpent said unto the woman, Ye shall not surely die:
Gen 3:5 For God doth know that in the day ye eat thereof, then your eyes shall be opened, and ye shall be as gods, knowing good and evil.
Gen 3:22 And the LORD God said, Behold, the man is become as one of us, to know good and evil: and now,

lest he put forth his hand, and take also of the tree of life, and eat, and live forever:

Gen 3:23 Therefore the LORD God sent him forth from the garden of Eden, to till the ground from whence he was taken.

Gen 3:24 So he drove out the man; and he placed at the east of the garden of Eden Cherubims, and a flaming sword which turned every way, to keep the way of the tree of life.

2Cr 3:18 But we all, with open face beholding as in a glass the glory of the Lord, are changed into the same image from glory to glory, [even] as by the Spirit of the Lord

Envy at the zenith, Satan is so much more than the archfiend. To spiritual beings the totality of loss is evident but we humans have but barely considered, do not know the enormity of what was done to us. Our mind is focused on details of this life. Humans were created in the image of God in spirit to live in flesh until sin cleaved His Spirit from us. When time is no more we will see in the volumes of the book of humanity the totality of evil that was perpetrated on us. The revelation will pierce the darkness that shocked Adam and Eve at the original sin and within all of us. At that moment humans will know the tragedy of our world throughout history. At that moment we will know who we are. At that moment we will know the grace of God Who is our loving Father.

Rev 10:6 And sware by him that liveth for ever and ever, who created heaven, and the things that therein are, and the earth, and the things that therein are, and the sea, and the things which are therein, that there should be time no longer:

Jhn 10:10 The thief cometh not, but for to steal, and to kill, and to destroy: I am come that they might have life, and that they might have [it] more abundantly.

Rom 6:23 For the wages of sin [is] death; but the gift of God [is] eternal life through Jesus Christ our Lord.
Luk 20:36 Neither can they die any more: for they are equal unto the angels; and are the children of God, being the children of the resurrection.
Eph 3:9 And to make all [men] see what [is] the fellowship of the mystery, which from the beginning of the world hath been hid in God, who created all things by Jesus Christ:
Eph 3:10 To the intent that now unto the principalities and powers in heavenly [places] might be known by the church the manifold wisdom of God,
Eph 3:11 According to the eternal purpose which he purposed in Christ Jesus our Lord:

Gen 2:25 and they were both naked, the man and his wife, and were not ashamed.
Gen 3:7 And the eyes of them both were opened, and they knew that they [were] naked; and they sewed fig leaves together, and made themselves aprons.
Gen 3:8 And they heard the voice of the LORD God walking in the garden in the cool of the day: and Adam and his wife hid themselves from the presence of the LORD God amongst the trees of the garden.

God was accustomed to "walk" in the garden. He shared in His creation with Adam and Eve.

Gen 3:9 And the LORD God called unto Adam, and said unto him, Where [art] thou?

God had regular conversation with Adam and Eve.

Gen 3:10 And he said, I heard thy voice in the garden, and I was afraid, because I [was] naked; and I hid myself.

Gen 3:11 And he said, Who told thee that thou [wast] naked? Hast thou eaten of the tree, whereof I commanded thee that thou shouldest not eat?

The book of Genesis is consistent. Focus concentrates intent into being. In this there is some sense of what Adam and Eve were before the fall and how they were naked, but not naked, by reason of focus. Their thought was other minded. God first asks Adam who told him he was naked.

Adam would not have known he was naked except that it was brought to his attention, or he had eaten the forbidden fruit which is the next question asked of Adam. Adam had lost the focus of God's will to the focus of his own will instead. Adam and Eve severed the Holy Spirit from their being. Who and what we are today have scarce time for God but are concerned with ourselves, I, me, mine, who, our replication vicariously in our children or preserved in our life's product/legacy. We do not have God's focus. Our race is not working to bring about the kingdom of God on Earth. Choices and opinions expressed in our world, our own lives today are not comfortable in God's kingdom. We are not ready to conform to God's will rather than our own choices or more accurately we do not choose God. We were truly separated at the decision against God in the garden. Those lives spent apart from God are entirely naked. They are wholly unprepared in every way for that which is to come as evidenced in panic and dread regarding death. They are naked of creative thoughts and heart where spirit, where God dwells.

Rev 3:17 Because thou sayest, I am rich, and increased with goods, and have need of nothing; and knowest not that thou art wretched, and miserable, and poor, and blind, and naked:
Luk 10:37 And he said, He that shewed mercy on him. Then said Jesus unto him, Go, and do thou likewise.

Mat 5:28 But I say unto you, That whosoever looketh on a woman to lust after her hath committed adultery with her already in his heart.
Luk 17:21 Neither shall they say, Lo here! or, lo there! for, behold, the kingdom of God is within you.
Gen 3:12 And the man said, The woman whom thou gavest [to be] with me, she gave me of the tree, and I did eat.
Gen 3:13 And the LORD God said unto the woman, What [is] this [that] thou hast done? And the woman said, The serpent beguiled me, and I did eat.

Perfect Irony, Humans are Saved by Death

Angels that sinned were cast into hell until the judgment. A difference between angels and humans reveals more of the purpose, the glory of God. Angels do not die. Humans die.

2Pe 2:4 For if God spared not the angels that sinned, but cast [them] down to hell, and delivered [them] into chains of darkness, to be reserved unto judgment;
2Pe 2:9 The Lord knoweth how to deliver the godly out of temptations, and to reserve the unjust unto the day of judgment to be punished:
Jud 1:6 And the angels which kept not their first estate, but left their own habitation, he hath reserved in everlasting chains under darkness unto the judgment of the great day.

Eze 18:4 Behold, all souls are mine; as the soul of the father, so also the soul of the son is mine: the soul that sinneth, it shall die.

Angels are reserved in everlasting chains until judgment because they do not die. Their imprisonment delivers the godly out of temptation. Human death confirms the word of

God yet proves the wisdom and glory of God. Death prevents the final fixture or the complete incorporation of sin, of error into the human being. Irony is perfect as death withstands human destruction. God stopped the fatal blow, the destruction of His human creation until the end of time where He will judge all. Satan intended sin and error to eradicate his human competition. Satan introduced sin into humans as evidence or a proof in validation of his contention with God. God has conquered sin and death. While humans live there is now the opportunity, forbearance, mercy, redemption and salvation to partake of the final element of the human creation that God will/does perform. In this, every human born into this life has a personal opportunity to choose God. The power of death executes the salvation of God for all who accept Him. Through death Jesus completed the perfect sacrifice expiating, redeeming His brethren.

Hbr 2:14 Forasmuch then as the children are partakers of flesh and blood, he also himself likewise took part of the same; that through death he might destroy him that had the power of death, that is, the devil;
Hbr 2:15 And deliver them who through fear of death were all their lifetime subject to bondage.
Hbr 2:16 For verily he took not on [him the nature of] angels; but he took on [him] the seed of Abraham.
Hbr 2:17 Wherefore in all things it behoved him to be made like unto [his] brethren, that he might be a merciful and faithful high priest in things [pertaining] to God, to make reconciliation for the sins of the people.
Hbr 2:18 For in that he himself hath suffered being tempted, he is able to succour them that are tempted.
1Cr 15:48 As [is] the earthy, such [are] they also that are earthy: and as [is] the heavenly, such [are] they also that are heavenly.
1Cr 15:49 And as we have borne the image of the earthy, we shall also bear the image of the heavenly.

1Cr 2:8 Which none of the princes of this world knew: for had they known [it], they would not have crucified the Lord of glory.

2Cr 5:21 For he hath made him [to be] sin for us, who knew no sin; that we might be made the righteousness of God in him.

Rom 8:2 For the law of the Spirit of life in Christ Jesus hath made me free from the law of sin and death.

Rom 8:6 For to be carnally minded [is] death; but to be spiritually minded [is] life and peace.

Rom 8:7 Because the carnal mind [is] enmity against God: for it is not subject to the law of God, neither indeed can be.

Rom 8:8 So then they that are in the flesh cannot please God.

Rom 8:9 But ye are not in the flesh, but in the Spirit, if so be that the Spirit of God dwell in you. Now if any man have not the Spirit of Christ, he is none of his.

Rom 8:10 And if Christ [be] in you, the body [is] dead because of sin; but the Spirit [is] life because of righteousness.

Rom 8:11 But if the Spirit of him that raised up Jesus from the dead dwell in you, he that raised up Christ from the dead shall also quicken your mortal bodies by his Spirit that dwelleth in you.

Rom 8:12 Therefore, brethren, we are debtors, not to the flesh, to live after the flesh.

Rom 8:13 For if ye live after the flesh, ye shall die: but if ye through the Spirit do mortify the deeds of the body, ye shall live.

Rom 8:14 For as many as are led by the Spirit of God, they are the sons of God.

Rom 8:15 For ye have not received the spirit of bondage again to fear; but ye have received the Spirit of adoption, whereby we cry, Abba, Father.

Rom 8:16 The Spirit itself beareth witness with our spirit, that we are the children of God:

Rom 8:17 And if children, then heirs; heirs of God, and joint-heirs with Christ; if so be that we suffer with [him], that we may be also glorified together.
Jam 4:4 Ye adulterers and adulteresses, know ye not that the friendship of the world is enmity with God? whosoever therefore will be a friend of the world is the enemy of God.
1Cr 15:50 Now this I say, brethren, that flesh and blood cannot inherit the kingdom of God; neither doth corruption inherit incorruption.
1Cr 15:51 Behold, I shew you a mystery; We shall not all sleep, but we shall all be changed,
1Cr 15:52 In a moment, in the twinkling of an eye, at the last trump: for the trumpet shall sound, and the dead shall be raised incorruptible, and we shall be changed.
1Cr 15:53 For this corruptible must put on incorruption, and this mortal [must] put on immortality.
1Cr 15:54 So when this corruptible shall have put on incorruption, and this mortal shall have put on immortality, then shall be brought to pass the saying that is written, Death is swallowed up in victory.
1Cr 15:55 O death, where [is] thy sting? O grave, where [is] thy victory?
1Cr 15:56 The sting of death [is] sin; and the strength of sin [is] the law.
1Cr 15:57 But thanks [be] to God, which giveth us the victory through our Lord Jesus Christ.

Afflicted Living

Gen 3:16 Unto the woman he said, I will greatly multiply thy sorrow and thy conception; in sorrow thou shalt bring forth children; and thy desire [shall be] to thy husband, and he shall rule over thee.

Eve's sorrow and conception are greatly multiplied, indicating that human being was to be a most different type of expression than we are accustomed to, who suffer the havoc of death. God's blessing to be fruitful and multiply has been subverted in a dire and sobering change. God knows the course of human being; His children who harm themselves by choice. Humans, all children of women, are now subject to the physical conditions of earthly life. Their choices align with or damage the life God had intended for them.

Women, our precious mothers are the gateway to enter this world. Life that is influenced at its source is more malleable for contrived purposes. For this reason Satan and other unbelievers are known to treat women harshly. Satan has directed his venom, his purpose to destroy us toward women from the beginning. Woman have been shamefully bullied and abused throughout history. Mothers withstand assaults directed at their lovingkindness, their sensitivity that is distinct to their being and essential for their reproduction of humans. Childbirth and rearing require much of mothers' lives. Care for their children can be an agonizing ordeal. Who suffers more as struggles or ills test her children? The loving half of our being, our mothers must be cherished.

Gen 3:17 And unto Adam he said, Because thou hast hearkened unto the voice of thy wife, and hast eaten of the tree, of which I commanded thee, saying, Thou shalt not eat of it: cursed [is] the ground for thy sake; in sorrow shalt thou eat [of] it all the days of thy life;
Gen 3:18 Thorns also and thistles shall it bring forth to thee; and thou shalt eat the herb of the field;
Gen 3:19 In the sweat of thy face shalt thou eat bread, till thou return unto the ground; for out of it wast thou taken: for dust thou [art], and unto dust shalt thou return.

Adam was formed of the dust of the Earth. Humans are henceforth tied to their choice, the conditions of their physical forms and the world that their choices now produce, the physical world absent the Spirit of God. These pronouncements could be considered judgments if one merely reads this small section of scripture and miss/take the Spirit of God. The first humans need to know how their manner of being will now change. Our Creator now must interact in a different manner with His creation.

Adam's first two responses of his own will were not very promising for the character of humanity. In the magnitude of godness, God must have been sorely disappointed. The Creator knew beyond the discordance of sin that subverted His creation, human being would inevitably become an expression of His image as His word exercises His purpose. The gift and bane of choice will prove those who are in the image of God. History documents sin inflicted atrocities among our ancestors. Our predecessors awakened each day to the same physical world of our experience. All suffer the abuse of sin yet pursue the affairs of life attainable within our hampered awareness. They prepared for each day as we too contemplate our daily schedules. In many places today human lives benefit from accumulated knowledge beyond those before us yet sin still wars throughout our world. Humanity suffers as the contention over belief obscures this dichotomy between the benefit of knowledge and the barbarism of sin. The elemental conflict to determine whether God or this world ultimately directs choice remains to be tested in every person's lifetime. The caress, bitterness, or philosophies of this world distract us from knowing. Lucifer was son of the morning, the anointed and covering cherub until his own behavior ended his occupation in those positions. Humans and angels will not escape the judgment of their own choices before God.

Eph 1:4 According as he hath chosen us in him before the foundation of the world, that we should be holy and without blame before him in love:
2Cr 4:4 In whom the god of this world hath blinded the minds of them which believe not, lest the light of

62

the glorious gospel of Christ, who is the image of God, should shine unto them.

Rom 12:2   And be not conformed to this world: but be ye transformed by the renewing of your mind, that ye may prove what [is] that good, and acceptable, and perfect, will of God.

Mar 4:13 And he said unto them, Know ye not this parable? and how then will ye know all parables?

Mar 4:14 The sower soweth the word.

Mar 4:15 And these are they by the way side, where the word is sown; but when they have heard, Satan cometh immediately, and taketh away the word that was sown in their hearts.

Mar 4:16 And these are they likewise which are sown on stony ground; who, when they have heard the word, immediately receive it with gladness;

Mar 4:17 And have no root in themselves, and so endure but for a time: afterward, when affliction or persecution ariseth for the word's sake, immediately they are offended.

Mar 4:18 And these are they which are sown among thorns; such as hear the word,

Mar 4:19 And the cares of this world, and the deceitfulness of riches, and the lusts of other things entering in, choke the word, and it becometh unfruitful.

Mar 4:20 And these are they which are sown on good ground; such as hear the word, and receive [it], and bring forth fruit, some thirtyfold, some sixty, and some an hundred.

Mar 4:21 And he said unto them, Is a candle brought to be put under a bushel, or under a bed? and not to be set on a candlestick?

Mar 4:22 For there is nothing hid, which shall not be manifested; neither was any thing kept secret, but that it should come abroad.

Mar 4:23 If any man have ears to hear, let him hear.

Mar 4:24 And he said unto them, Take heed what ye hear: with what measure ye mete, it shall be measured to you: and unto you that hear shall more be given.
Mar 4:25 For he that hath, to him shall be given: and he that hath not, from him shall be taken even that which he hath.

Willfulness

The challenge to His will, against His expressed purpose will not prevail. Humans being in the image of God will inhabit all of His blessings and promises living within His presence. Discordance, violation, the sour note and offense that the appearance of Satan and then Cain inflicted were subtle and brutal abuses and were severe insertions that plainly are out of place even upon a person's first reading of these events. These acts are so contrary they cause confusion; a disconnection with the story.

The book of Genesis is a bitter display of human conduct. Twice humans were given a new world to cultivate and prosper before and after the flood. In this God silenced any contention that human pride was denied opportunity. The word of God will accomplish His purpose but now human creation will be done the hard way. The ground and all of our products must henceforth be tended to overcome the harm caused by contradiction. There is now interfering contamination and contention of earth's and humanity's fruits. Daughters and sons of Adam must work now to accomplish the requirements resulting from their choices. Human choice is a test of being, of what one will become.

Abhorrent beyond any extreme tragedy animal or physical elements can inflict is the betrayal; the cruelty humans inflict within the family among the children of God. The transition from what they were, the family of God and lords of the earth is most traumatic indeed. Betrayal, cruelty, murder, rape, slander, slavery, theft, torture, warfare are only a few examples of the rupture from the will of God. Kindness and love are sorely tested confronting evil that will not be dissuaded. Despite what we may desire, choice proves creation or damnation.

Isa 55:8 For my thoughts [are] not your thoughts, neither [are] your ways my ways, saith the LORD.
Rom 12:17 Recompense to no man evil for evil. Provide things honest in the sight of all men.
Rom 12:18 If it be possible, as much as lieth in you, live peaceably with all men.
Rom 12:19 Dearly beloved, avenge not yourselves, but [rather] give place unto wrath: for it is written, Vengeance [is] mine; I will repay, saith the Lord.
Rom 12:20 Therefore if thine enemy hunger, feed him; if he thirst, give him drink: for in so doing thou shalt heap coals of fire on his head.
Rom 12:21 Be not overcome of evil, but overcome evil with good.
Mat 25:31 When the Son of man shall come in his glory, and all the holy angels with him, then shall he sit upon the throne of his glory:
Mat 25:32 and before him shall be gathered all nations: and he shall separate them one from another, as a shepherd divideth [his] sheep from the goats:
Mat 25:33 and he shall set the sheep on his right hand, but the goats on the left.
Mat 25:34 Then shall the King say unto them on his right hand, Come, ye blessed of my Father, inherit the kingdom prepared for you from the foundation of the world:

As with our birth, we acquire responsibilities accounted to us that were outside of our volition. Some of what we are is preprogrammed apart from what might have been given the choice. Our first ancestors ate the fruit of the tree of the knowledge of good and evil in disobedience to God's command. We exist within this sin imposed dilemma, the first humans were created from the dust, humans reproduce after their kind, on the earth and flesh and blood cannot enter heaven. All life in this world dies. There remains a tree of life inaccessible to physical efforts. The decision is confirmed by the action. Disobedience is the outward manifestation of a person's skepticism, their unbelief. The majority agent of the human condition in Genesis is disobedience.

From the first human sin forward God's unheeded warning was proven correct, humans surely die. The Creator will exercise preference but was God cursing humans or proclaiming the reality of their new existence? God's intention is more evident when He acquires a human body to save His children.

Jhn 3:16 For God so loved the world, that he gave his only begotten Son, that whosoever believeth in him should not perish, but have everlasting life.
Mat 26:39 And he went a little further, and fell on his face, and prayed, saying, O my Father, if it be possible, let this cup pass from me: nevertheless not as I will, but as thou [wilt].
Mat 26:42 He went away again the second time, and prayed, saying, O my Father, if this cup may not pass away from me, except I drink it, thy will be done.
Jhn 5:30 I can of mine own self do nothing: as I hear, I judge: and my judgment is just; because I seek not mine own will, but the will of the Father which hath sent me.

Confirmation of Truth

Humanity is a bloody record of the wages of sin. Undeniably, the life of the flesh is the blood. The power of blood, in writing, spoken about or seen cannot be denied in any level of our awareness, it is life. The blood of all those to be slain was of no consequence to Satan the liar as he said to Eve, you shall not surely die. Satan exercised his mature knowledge to alter naïve, naked Adam and Eve's existence. Satan's condescension, his manner, in fact the one most supremely self absorbed and disdainful of humans himself magnified the pain of his sentence for despoiling the glory and purpose of God's human creation.

Gen 3:15 And I will put enmity between thee and the woman, and between thy seed and her seed; it shall bruise thy head, and thou shalt bruise his heel.

Gen 4:10 And he said, What hast thou done? the voice of thy brother's blood crieth unto me from the ground.

Gen 4:11 And now [art] thou cursed from the earth, which hath opened her mouth to receive thy brother's blood from thy hand;

Gen 9:6 Whoso sheddeth man's blood, by man shall his blood be shed: for in the image of God made he man.

Lev 17:11 For the life of the flesh [is] in the blood: and I have given it to you upon the altar to make an atonement for your souls: for it [is] the blood [that] maketh an atonement for the soul.

Lev 17:14 For [it is] the life of all flesh; the blood of it [is] for the life thereof: therefore I said unto the children of Israel, Ye shall eat the blood of no manner of flesh: for the life of all flesh [is] the blood thereof: whosoever eateth it shall be cut off.

Luk 11:48 Truly ye bear witness that ye allow the deeds of your fathers: for they indeed killed them, and ye build their sepulchres.

Luk 11:49Therefore also said the wisdom of God, I will send them prophets and apostles, and [some] of them they shall slay and persecute:

Luk 11:50That the blood of all the prophets, which was shed from the foundation of the world, may be required of this generation;

Luk 11:51 From the blood of Abel unto the blood of Zacharias, which perished between the altar and the

temple: verily I say unto you, It shall be required of this generation.
Luk 22:19 And he took bread, and gave thanks, and brake [it], and gave unto them, saying, This is my body which is given for you: this do in remembrance of me.
Luk 22:20 Likewise also the cup after supper, saying, This cup [is] the new testament in my blood, which is shed for you.
Hbr 9:22 And almost all things are by the law purged with blood; and without shedding of blood is no remission.
Jhn 6:53 Then Jesus said unto them, Verily, verily, I say unto you, Except ye eat the flesh of the Son of man, and drink his blood, ye have no life in you.
Jhn 6:54 Whoso eateth my flesh, and drinketh my blood, hath eternal life; and I will raise him up at the last day.

Sacrifice of Blood for Life

The blood of Jesus, just as His Being here on Earth was both God and human, physical and spiritual is our redemption. It is redemption by His choice to gift through His sacrificial death literally, and figuratively life. His life was physical as was His pain and suffering yet was and is spiritual. We now may receive His Spirit, His life.

Gal 4:4 But when the fulness of the time was come, God sent forth his Son, made of a woman, made under the law,
Gal 4:5 To redeem them that were under the law, that we might receive the adoption of sons.
Rom 9:4 Who are Israelites; to whom [pertaineth] the adoption, and the glory, and the covenants, and the giving of the law, and the service [of God], and the promises;

Rom 9:5 Whose [are] the fathers, and of whom as concerning the flesh Christ [came], who is over all, God blessed for ever. Amen.
Rom 9:6 Not as though the word of God hath taken none effect. For they [are] not all Israel, which are of Israel:
Rom 9:7 Neither, because they are the seed of Abraham, [are they] all children: but, In Isaac shall thy seed be called.
Rom 9:8 That is, They which are the children of the flesh, these [are] not the children of God: but the children of the promise are counted for the seed.
Rom 2:14 For when the Gentiles, which have not the law, do by nature the things contained in the law, these, having not the law, are a law unto themselves:
Rom 4:13 For the promise, that he should be the heir of the world, [was] not to Abraham, or to his seed, through the law, but through the righteousness of faith.
Rom 4:14 For if they which are of the law [be] heirs, faith is made void, and the promise made of none effect:
Rom 4:15 Because the law worketh wrath: for where no law is, [there is] no transgression.
Rom 4:16 Therefore [it is] of faith, that [it might be] by grace; to the end the promise might be sure to all the seed; not to that only which is of the law, but to that also which is of the faith of Abraham; who is the father of us all,
Gal 4:6 And because ye are sons, God hath sent forth the Spirit of his Son into your hearts, crying, Abba, Father.
Gal 4:7 Wherefore thou art no more a servant, but a son; and if a son, then an heir of God through Christ.
Gal 4:8 Howbeit then, when ye knew not God, ye did service unto them which by nature are no gods.

Pro 8:36 but he that sinneth against me wrongeth his own soul: all they that hate me love death.
Jam 5:20 Let him know, that he which converteth the sinner from the error of his way shall save a soul from death, and shall hide a multitude of sins.
Hbr 5:7 Who in the days of his flesh, when he had offered up prayers and supplications with strong crying and tears unto him that was able to save him from death, and was heard in that he feared;
Hbr 5:8 Though he were a Son, yet learned he obedience by the things which he suffered;
Hbr 5:9 And being made perfect, he became the author of eternal salvation unto all them that obey him;
2Cr 5:18 and all things [are] of God, who hath reconciled us to Himself by Jesus Christ, and hath given to us the ministry of reconciliation;
2Cr 5:19 To wit, that God was in Christ, reconciling the world unto Himself, not imputing their trespasses unto them; and hath committed unto us the word of reconciliation.
2Cr 5:20 Now then we are ambassadors for Christ, as though God did beseech [you] by us: we pray [you] in Christ's stead, be ye reconciled to God.
2Cr 5:21 For he hath made him [to be] sin for us, who knew no sin; that we might be made the righteousness of God in him.
Jhn 14:16 And I will pray the Father, and he shall give you another Comforter, that he may abide with you for ever;
Jhn 14:17 [Even] the Spirit of truth; whom the world cannot receive, because it seeth him not, neither knoweth him: but ye know him; for he dwelleth with you, and shall be in you.
Jhn 14:18 I will not leave you comfortless: I will come to you.

2Pe 3:9 The Lord is not slack concerning his promise, as some men count slackness; but is longsuffering to us-ward, not willing that any should perish, but that all should come to repentance.

Rev 3:18 I counsel thee to buy of me gold tried in the fire, that thou mayest be rich; and white raiment, that thou mayest be clothed, and [that] the shame of thy nakedness do not appear; and anoint thine eyes with eyesalve, that thou mayest see.

Act 3:19 Repent ye therefore, and be converted, that your sins may be blotted out, when the times of refreshing shall come from the presence of the Lord;

Act 3:20 And he shall send Jesus Christ, which before was preached unto you:

Act 3:21 Whom the heaven must receive until the times of restitution of all things, which God hath spoken by the mouth of all his holy prophets since the world began.

Gen 3:20 And Adam called his wife's name Eve; because she was the mother of all living.

Gen 3:21 Unto Adam also and to his wife did the LORD God make coats of skins, and clothed them.

Chapter 4
A Garden with Trees

In the beginning, the creation bending decision to partake of the tree of the knowledge of good and evil, the vital essence of the tree of life, coupled with the frequency that trees are mentioned confirms the intended emphasis of trees. Apart from God, only earth and man are mentioned more than tree. Trees produce oxygen, lift water into the clouds, produce food, provide materials for construction, record conditions of each year and process decaying matter into fertile soil. Trees are a gift, a standard of benefit and are apt examples that are known to every culture or era of human existence. As with other instances where the bible identifies specific persons, places and things there is much to be known of the tree.

Gen 2:8 And the LORD God planted a garden eastward in Eden; and there he put the man whom he had formed.
Gen 2:9 And out of the ground made the LORD God to grow every tree that is pleasant to the sight, and good for food; the tree of life also in the midst of the garden, and the tree of knowledge of good and evil.
Gen 2:15 And the LORD God took the man, and put him into the garden of Eden to dress it and to keep it.
Gen 2:16 And the LORD God commanded the man, saying, of every tree of the garden thou mayest freely eat:
Gen 2:17 But of the tree of the knowledge of good and evil, thou shalt not eat of it: for in the day that thou eatest thereof thou shalt surely die.
Gen 2:25 And they were both naked, the man and his wife, and were not ashamed.

Genesis describes trees.

Gen 1:11 And God said, Let the earth bring forth grass, the herb yielding seed, [and] the fruit tree yielding fruit after his kind, whose seed [is] in itself, upon the earth: and it was so.
Gen 1:12 And the earth brought forth grass, [and] herb yielding seed after his kind, and the tree yielding fruit, whose seed [was] in itself, after his kind: and God saw that [it was] good.

There is an emphasis on tree as a type that is described in 2 successive versus in the first chapter. (Genesis 1:11 and 1:12) "the fruit tree yielding fruit after his kind, whose seed [is] in itself, upon the earth " and "the tree yielding fruit, whose seed [was] in itself, after his kind"

A list from the Genesis tree type has these 4 characteristics:
1. Yields fruit,
2. Whose seed is in itself
3. After his kind
4. Upon the earth

These characteristics can be expected from many living things of the earth and are typical. Genesis is the revelation of creation and the types created. Trees are consistent, constant in the created purpose and are stalwart guides to being and living parables.

Psa 1:3 And he shall be like a tree planted by the rivers of water, that bringeth forth his fruit in his season; his leaf also shall not wither; and whatsoever he doeth shall prosper.
Mat 12:33 Either make the tree good, and his fruit good; or else make the tree corrupt, and his fruit corrupt: for the tree is known by [his] fruit.

Mat 12:34 O generation of vipers, how can ye, being evil, speak good things? for out of the abundance of the heart the mouth speaketh.

Mat 12:35 A good man out of the good treasure of the heart bringeth forth good things: and an evil man out of the evil treasure bringeth forth evil things.

Mat 12:36 But I say unto you, That every idle word that men shall speak, they shall give account thereof in the day of judgment.

Mat 12:37 For by thy words thou shalt be justified, and by thy words thou shalt be condemned.

Mar 7:15 There is nothing from without a man that entering into him can defile him: but the things which come out of him, those are they that defile the man.

Mar 7:16 If any man have ears to hear, let him hear.

Mar 7:17 And when he was entered into the house from the people, his disciples asked him concerning the parable.

Mar 7:18 And he saith unto them, Are ye so without understanding also? Do ye not perceive, that whatsoever thing from without entereth into the man, [it] cannot defile him;

Mar 7:19 Because it entereth not into his heart, but into the belly, and goeth out into the draught, purging all meats?

Mar 7:20 And he said, That which cometh out of the man, that defileth the man.

Mar 7:21 For from within, out of the heart of men, proceed evil thoughts, adulteries, fornications, murders,

Mar 7:22 Thefts, covetousness, wickedness, deceit, lasciviousness, an evil eye, blasphemy, pride, foolishness:

Mar 7:23 All these evil things come from within, and defile the man.

Luk 6:45 A good man out of the good treasure of his heart bringeth forth that which is good; and an evil man out of the evil treasure of his heart bringeth forth that which is evil: for of the abundance of the heart his mouth speaketh.

Jam 3:8 But the tongue can no man tame; [it is] an unruly evil, full of deadly poison.
Jam 3:9 Therewith bless we God, even the Father; and therewith curse we men, which are made after the similitude of God.
Jam 3:10 Out of the same mouth proceedeth blessing and cursing. My brethren, these things ought not so to be.
Jam 3:11 Doth a fountain send forth at the same place sweet [water] and bitter?
Jam 3:12 Can the fig tree, my brethren, bear olive berries? either a vine, figs? so [can] no fountain both yield salt water and fresh.
Jam 3:13 Who [is] a wise man and endued with knowledge among you? let him shew out of a good conversation his works with meekness of wisdom.
Jam 3:14 But if ye have bitter envying and strife in your hearts, glory not, and lie not against the truth.
Jam 3:15 This wisdom descendeth not from above, but [is] earthly, sensual, devilish.
Jam 3:16 For where envying and strife [is], there [is] confusion and every evil work.
Jam 3:17 But the wisdom that is from above is first pure, then peaceable, gentle, [and] easy to be intreated, full of mercy and good fruits, without partiality, and without hypocrisy.
Jam 3:18 And the fruit of righteousness is sown in peace of them that make peace.
Gal 6:8 For he that soweth to his flesh shall of the flesh reap corruption; but he that soweth to the Spirit shall of the Spirit reap life everlasting.

Rom 11:16 For if the firstfruit [be] holy, the lump [is] also [holy]: and if the root [be] holy, so [are] the branches.

Rom 11:17 And if some of the branches be broken off, and thou, being a wild olive tree, wert graffed in among them, and with them partakest of the root and fatness of the olive tree;

Rom 11:18 Boast not against the branches. But if thou boast, thou bearest not the root, but the root thee.

Rom 11:19 Thou wilt say then, the branches were broken off, that I might be grafted in.

Rom 11:20 Well; because of unbelief they were broken off, and thou standest by faith. Be not highminded, but fear:

Rom 11:21 For if God spared not the natural branches, [take heed] lest he also spare not thee.

Rom 11:22 Behold therefore the goodness and severity of God: on them which fell, severity; but toward thee, goodness, if thou continue in [his] goodness: otherwise thou also shalt be cut off.

Rom 11:23 And they also, if they abide not still in unbelief, shall be graffed in: for God is able to graff them in again.

Rom 11:24 For if thou wert cut out of the olive tree which is wild by nature, and wert graffed contrary to nature into a good olive tree: how much more shall these, which be the natural [branches], be graffed into their own olive tree?

Isa 61:3 To appoint unto them that mourn in Zion, to give unto them beauty for ashes, the oil of joy for mourning, the garment of praise for the spirit of heaviness; that they might be called trees of righteousness, the planting of the LORD, that he might be glorified.

Tree of Life

The tree of life is one of only two remarkable trees in the garden. These 2 trees are unknown to us but for the biblical references. The tree of life is found 10 times in this scripture, 3 in Genesis, 4 in Proverbs and 3 times in Revelation.   The tree of life is contrary to our common lives, considered as both fable and fabulous being outside of our experience and yet much to be desired. These characteristics are some of the qualities of biblical revelation in contrast to the human condition thereby strange and hard to accept for many.

Today we are housed, nourished and restored or augmented by trees. There are at least 120 drugs obtained from trees that are used to affect our being. These effects are temporary for our purposes unless applied to end a life.   None of these drugs were readily useful before discovery or investigation prepared them for our uses. Ignorance is certain before revelation. The tree of life is regarded as no more than fable as it is not present and is unattainable in our lives. Rational approaches to scripture are foiled by revelations such as the tree of life. This tree is more palatable as a metaphor for such minds yet this convention becomes an irrational assignment for the multitude of fabulous beings, events and objects in the bible. The Creator is not limited to our means and understanding or the bible is only a collection of pre science explanations of the unknown.

Tree of the Knowledge of Good and Evil

The tree of the knowledge of good and evil is specifically named only twice and alluded to 5 additional times in Genesis. The tree of the knowledge of good and evil is discounted as fable. The knowledge of good and evil is in us. We do not acquire it. Our self-assurance will not believe that it came from a tree that is unknown to us. It is assumed to be part of human being. This tree could also be known as the tree of the knowledge of "who". Planted into humanity with the forbidden taking, that seed immediately began to produce fruit. After all, it is named the tree of the knowledge of "good" and "evil". There was no further need to express the potential, the fruit was manifest. The effect of this tree is so certain mention of this specifically named tree does not escape the third chapter of Genesis.

Absolute, irrevocable measures are cessation of the former condition or state of existence. A fruit of potency and vigor sufficient to permanently alter our being is scripturally depicted in a single instance of ingestion into each human component of reproduction. How smug Satan is in our world conception. We do not consider or perceive that which has not been discovered or produced by us. As a child knows no other manner of parental behavior than that received from their own, so do we presume our life's condition. Our self-confidence is a component that limits our perception of our true being. We are tragic in ignorance, satisfied in our exclusive abilities. Déjà vu has a peculiar sparkle for us that is not reckoned as anything more than an apt convention for a story. Actually, our hitch on the concept comes from our curtailed perception. There should be no perplexity that the same sins are repeated almost in a mirror of one's own actions. We do not understand and are then relegated to continue in sin and error because we the human image, prefer an advantage, just like sin too much to acquire the dignity God intends of His human creation. The dignity that is precious to continue, to live in creation while manifesting the fruits of true life.

"Who" is a double edged sword and utmost in the accuser of the brethren, Satan's thoughts. Satan was in the garden but not of the garden. Lucifer was removed from heaven as he became too self consumed for the position. Adam and Eve hid but their choice, their persons, aware of who and nakedness no longer aligned with the garden. It was impossible for them to hide as they no longer were of the garden. Their minds became contrary to God. Here, creation explores the irony of the marriage of spirit and flesh accomplished in the comingling of these two disparate elements. God will reveal more of His intent for humans but clearly it was creation, not corruption. The human spectacle eventually will manifest the purpose and glory of God.

Rom 7:25 I thank God through Jesus Christ our Lord. So then with the mind I myself serve the law of God; but with the flesh the law of sin.

Rom 8:7 Because the carnal mind [is] enmity against God: for it is not subject to the law of God, neither indeed can be.

Gen 3:22 and the LORD God said, behold, the man is become as one of us, to know good and evil: and now, lest he put forth his hand, and take also of the tree of life, and eat, and live for ever:

Gen 3:23 Therefore the LORD God sent him forth from the garden of Eden, to till the ground from whence he was taken.

Gen 3:24 So he drove out the man; and he placed at the east of the garden of Eden Cherubims, and a flaming sword which turned every way, to keep the way of the tree of life.

Rom 8:27 And he that searcheth the hearts knoweth what [is] the mind of the Spirit, because he maketh intercession for the saints according to [the will of] God.

Rom 12:2 And be not conformed to this world: but be ye transformed by the renewing of your mind, that ye may prove what [is] that good, and acceptable, and perfect, will of God.

Rom 15:6 That ye may with one mind [and] one mouth glorify God, even the Father of our Lord Jesus Christ.

2Cr 13:11 Finally, brethren, farewell. Be perfect, be of good comfort, be of one mind, live in peace; and the God of love and peace shall be with you.

Col 3:12 Put on therefore, as the elect of God, holy and beloved, bowels of mercies, kindness, humbleness of mind, meekness, longsuffering;
2Ti 1:7 For God hath not given us the spirit of fear; but of power, and of love, and of a sound mind.
Hbr 8:10 For this [is] the covenant that I will make with the house of Israel after those days, saith the Lord; I will put my laws into their mind, and write them in their hearts: and I will be to them a God, and they shall be to me a people:

God is true. Confirmation of the truth was too stark, too sudden in Cain. There is no maybe in corruption. We assume and reserve our own personal lives apart from the evil of others. Humans worldwide participate in the deception blaming happenstance, business, disease, government, intoxication, religion, peoples and natural disasters for poverty, bullying, defamation, theft, warfare, enslavement and all other instances of human suffering. Theories of behavior and creation prove the human denial of and unwillingness to consider our creator.

Rom 3:10 As it is written, There is none righteous, no, not one:
Rom 3:11 There is none that understandeth, there is none that seeketh after God.
Rom 3:12 They are all gone out of the way, they are together become unprofitable; there is none that doeth good, no, not one.

All of the beginning is swift and in sharp contrast. The explosive intent, the correctness to create was effected in just seven days including rest. In short order all are named. We were created, tempted and are corrupted. Human focus, choices, our being cannot partake of the precious fruit of the garden. The tree of life is alive in scripture but not to our knowing. Potential holds out to elicit wonder unto repentance.

The tree of life awaits for all who, "call upon the name of the LORD", to those who focus on the will of God.

Jam 4:1 From whence [come] wars and fightings among you? [come they] not hence, [even] of your lusts that war in your members?
Jam 4:2 Ye lust, and have not: ye kill, and desire to have, and cannot obtain: ye fight and war, yet ye have not, because ye ask not.
Jam 4:3 Ye ask, and receive not, because ye ask amiss, that ye may consume [it] upon your lusts.
Jam 4:4 Ye adulterers and adulteresses, know ye not that the friendship of the world is enmity with God? whosoever therefore will be a friend of the world is the enemy of God.
Jam 4:5 Do ye think that the scripture saith in vain, The spirit that dwelleth in us lusteth to envy?
Jam 4:6 But he giveth more grace. Wherefore he saith, God resisteth the proud, but giveth grace unto the humble.
Jam 4:7 Submit yourselves therefore to God. Resist the devil, and he will flee from you.
Jam 4:8 Draw nigh to God, and he will draw nigh to you. Cleanse [your] hands, [ye] sinners; and purify [your] hearts, [ye] double minded.
Jam 4:9 Be afflicted, and mourn, and weep: let your laughter be turned to mourning, and [your] joy to heaviness.
Jam 4:10 Humble yourselves in the sight of the Lord, and he shall lift you up.
Jam 3:2 For in many things we offend all. If any man offend not in word, the same [is] a perfect man, [and] able also to bridle the whole body.
1Pe 5:5 Likewise, ye younger, submit yourselves unto the elder. Yea, all [of you] be subject one to another, and be clothed with humility: for God resisteth the proud, and giveth grace to the humble.

Eph 4:13 Till we all come in the unity of the faith, and of the knowledge of the Son of God, unto a perfect man, unto the measure of the stature of the fulness of Christ:

Col 1:28 Whom we preach, warning every man, and teaching every man in all wisdom; that we may present every man perfect in Christ Jesus:

2Ti 3:15 And that from a child thou hast known the holy scriptures, which are able to make thee wise unto salvation through faith which is in Christ Jesus.

2Ti 3:16 All scripture [is] given by inspiration of God, and [is] profitable for doctrine, for reproof, for correction, for instruction in righteousness:

2Ti 3:17 That the man of God may be perfect, throughly furnished unto all good works.

Jam 1:25 But whoso looketh into the perfect law of liberty, and continueth [therein], he being not a forgetful hearer, but a doer of the work, this man shall be blessed in his deed.

Chapter 5
Look Here

The Genesis early chapters' manner of explanation is contrary to us who are captives to time. While at a time, yet apart from time, creation appears. Biblical revelation is occasionally unmindful of time and related apart from our pattern of thought especially at creation. The first time is precedent and yet arrives from the insubstantial. Now the One outside of time imparts understanding to beings in time.

2Pe 3:8 But, beloved, be not ignorant of this one thing, that one day [is] with the Lord as a thousand years, and a thousand years as one day.

Time exists for those who die. Death mocks every human endeavor; it haunts our hopes and dreams. The human race is descriptive of our lives as well as our species. We run out of time. Await, daily, deadline, delay, expedite, holiday, hourly, imprison, legacy, leisure, memorial, procrastinate, reminisce, retire, rush, schedule, vacation, years, are a few of the words with us due to the adamant limitation of this physical existence. How very dear the loss of time becomes as life wanes for residents of this planet. Loss is the reality of the latter years of life. No amount of wealth can purchase an extension. Sorrow for the loss can overwhelm the staunchest control. Lifespan conforms and effects thought. Schools, written and digital media are time management structures that steer and prepare youth and the student's emergence and also convey experiences to others; to transcend distance, eras and epochs. Institutions and devices assist the transfer and growth of knowledge for short lived humans who are nevertheless mired in time deprived conceptualization. Our calendars and schedules portray this human condition. Days are components of our limitation and shackles affecting the awareness of earthbound mortals.

Gen 6:3 And the LORD said, My spirit shall not always strive with man, for that he also [is] flesh: yet his days shall be an hundred and twenty years.

We have feeble knowledge of the lives of notables who lived only 2 thousand years ago. Knowledge of everyday life in that era is gleaned from the shards and scraps that remain. Earlier cultures are subject to conjecture that distorts and maims our understanding of the actual motives and causal influences. History is not so much the victim as our personal understanding, our life's direction that is diminished by naiveté'. Pre flood humans lived more than 10 of our lives. They would not need to preserve history, they lived history. Those people would have been very powerful not merely due to superb bodies but conceive of the exponention of knowledge. Lifespans presented in Genesis 5 are examples of biblical revelation that contradict our own life condition. We are perplexed by amazing ancient edifices that spawn all manner of theories. All that has been attained in this current era would vanish in an instant war of the invisible electromagnetic pulse. A worldwide flood compounded the erasure of living history contained in each person with the additional physical devastation of structures. The eradication of people, societies, history, structures and the reduction of life spans to 120 years severely impeded any recovery of the pre flood civilizations effectively redirecting the course of human development. Humans lost all their former grandeur in this actual extinction event. The Creator did not choose to begin again with a new being. The Almighty preserved 8 people as the expression of His purpose to create man in His image and likeness. There is this hole in our understanding of how we are that is incongruent with the evident ancient wisdom. The disjointed scraps of archeological pieces cannot be coaxed into a solution to the puzzle. Our short lifetime narrows our focus to a personal journey. Short lives are more concerned with details than with whole or eternal considerations. Life is treasure owned by each breathing person, treasure greater than gold or any other measure of earth dweller wealth. Life is beyond human means.

Eph 5:13 But all things that are reproved are made manifest by the light: for whatsoever doth make manifest is light.
Eph 5:14 Wherefore he saith, Awake thou that sleepest, and arise from the dead, and Christ shall give thee light.
Eph 5:15 See then that ye walk circumspectly, not as fools, but as wise,
Eph 5:16 Redeeming the time, because the days are evil.

There is but one mention of the birth of a woman in the first four chapters of Genesis although wives accompany each man. Here follows another difference of perception between physical beings and spiritual.

Gen 5:1 This [is] the book of the generations of Adam. In the day that God created man, in the likeness of God made He him;
Gen 5:2 Male and female created He them; and blessed them, and called their name Adam, in the day when they were created.

Further revelation of the effects of sin is first introduced by the spiritual perception of Adam, male and female in the first 2 verses of chapter 5. God, Who addresses people according to what they are, refers to the male and female as Adam. This glimpse of the spiritual conception of the physical repeats the generalized view of that which we humans within creation see with more detail. The second post sin question asked of Adam, "Who told you that you were naked?" is insightful of Adam and Eve's pre sin focus, evidence of a more spiritual focus of a different mind. Creation of the Earth is completed in the first chapter, but then more detail follows in the second for our benefit who, without spirit cannot know as spirit does. Adam and Eve were unnamed for a while but became more who after the forbidden indulgence. Creation does not end with the generation of Adam and Eve. The manner of being, methods and customs, including even the physical world were and still are under construction. Human being is self confined in the narrowed focus of detail. The physical coalesces around thought. This is an instance of how human is in the image of God, thought generates physical and spiritual occurrence. Creation is to be continued by human being in the image of God.

Gen 11:6 And the LORD said, Behold, the people [is] one, and they have all one language; and this they begin to do: and now nothing will be restrained from them, which they have imagined to do.
Deu 23:23 That which is gone out of thy lips thou shalt keep and perform; [even] a freewill offering, according as thou hast vowed unto the LORD thy God, which thou hast promised with thy mouth.
Mat 12:36 But I say unto you, That every idle word that men shall speak, they shall give account thereof in the day of judgment.
Hbr 11:1 Now faith is the substance of things hoped for, the evidence of things not seen.
Hbr 11:2 For by it the elders obtained a good report.
Hbr 11:3 Through faith we understand that the worlds were framed by the word of God, so that things which are seen were not made of things which do appear.
1Th 5:17 Pray without ceasing.

Think to do

Genesis recognizes specific people who contrast truth through their activities. The physical beings are now aware of who and by nature more aware of sex and call themselves humans. The spiritual realm in contrast is asexual. Human duality is one tension to be tested and proven in the human display that is of more consequence as desire increases within the human experience. Thought is much more the creative process than can be comfortably admitted in retrospection of our lives.

Thought, decision and action behave like the trunk, sap and branches of our mindful tree to deliver the fruit of our considerations. Choice is provided a vessel for a limited lifetime. A lifetime is an awakening, learning, and gradually becoming the expression of choices. Given the physical conditions of this world there is scarce encouragement for selfless behavior apart from that provided by revelation from God. Thoughts aligned with God, or with self are evident.

Mat 6:21 For where your treasure is, there will your heart be also.
1Cr 15:46 Howbeit that [was] not first which is spiritual, but that which is natural; and afterward that which is spiritual.
Rom 6:16 Know ye not, that to whom ye yield yourselves servants to obey, his servants ye are to whom ye obey; whether of sin unto death, or of obedience unto righteousness?
Rom 7:18 For I know that in me (that is, in my flesh,) dwelleth no good thing: for to will is present with me; but [how] to perform that which is good I find not.
Rom 7:19 For the good that I would I do not: but the evil which I would not, that I do.
Rom 7:20 Now if I do that I would not, it is no more I that do it but sin that dwelleth in me.
Rom 7:21 I find then a law, that, when I would do good, evil is present with me.
Rom 7:22 For I delight in the law of God after the inward man:
Rom 7:23 But I see another law in my members, warring against the law of my mind, and bringing me into captivity to the law of sin which is in my members.
Rom 7:24 O wretched man that I am! who shall deliver me from the body of this death?
Rom 7:25 I thank God through Jesus Christ our Lord. So then with the mind I myself serve the law of God; but with the flesh the law of sin.

Jer 9:24 But let him that glorieth glory in this, that he understandeth and knoweth me, that I [am] the LORD which exercise lovingkindness, judgment, and righteousness, in the earth: for in these [things] I delight, saith the LORD.
Phl 4:8 Finally, brethren, whatsoever things are true, whatsoever things [are] honest, whatsoever things [are] just, whatsoever things [are] pure, whatsoever things [are] lovely, whatsoever things [are] of good report; if [there be] any virtue, and if [there be] any praise, think on these things.

Corruption was swift with Cain but is also gradual and insidious. Thought is the creative process. Contemplation extends out beyond precipices endangering not merely the unbeliever but whole societies.

Mat 13:33 Another parable spake he unto them; The kingdom of heaven is like unto leaven, which a woman took, and hid in three measures of meal, till the whole was leavened.
Mat 16:11 How is it that ye do not understand that I spake [it] not to you concerning bread, that ye should beware of the leaven of the Pharisees and of the Sadducees?
Mat 16:12 Then understood they how that he bade [them] not beware of the leaven of bread, but of the doctrine of the Pharisees and of the Sadducees.
1Cr 5:6 Your glorying [is] not good. Know ye not that a little leaven leaveneth the whole lump?
1Cr 5:7 Purge out therefore the old leaven, that ye may be a new lump, as ye are unleavened. For even Christ our passover is sacrificed for us:
1Cr 5:8 Therefore let us keep the feast, not with old leaven, neither with the leaven of malice and wickedness; but with the unleavened [bread] of sincerity and truth.

1Cr 5:9 I wrote unto you in an epistle not to company with fornicators:

1Cr 5:10 Yet not altogether with the fornicators of this world, or with the covetous, or extortioners, or with idolaters; for then must ye needs go out of the world.

1Cr 5:11 But now I have written unto you not to keep company, if any man that is called a brother be a fornicator, or covetous, or an idolater, or a railer, or a drunkard, or an extortioner; with such an one no not to eat.

Luk 12:1 In the mean time, when there were gathered together an innumerable multitude of people, insomuch that they trode one upon another, he began to say unto his disciples first of all, Beware ye of the leaven of the Pharisees, which is hypocrisy.

Luk 12:2 For there is nothing covered, that shall not be revealed; neither hid, that shall not be known.

Luk 12:3 Therefore whatsoever ye have spoken in darkness shall be heard in the light; and that which ye have spoken in the ear in closets shall be proclaimed upon the housetops.

Luk 12:4 And I say unto you my friends, Be not afraid of them that kill the body, and after that have no more that they can do.

Luk 12:5 But I will forewarn you whom ye shall fear: Fear Him, which after He hath killed hath power to cast into hell; yea, I say unto you, Fear Him.

2Ti 3:1 This know also, that in the last days perilous times shall come.

2Ti 3:2 for men shall be lovers of their own selves, covetous, boasters, proud, blasphemers, disobedient to parents, unthankful, unholy,

2Ti 3:3 without natural affection, trucebreakers, false accusers, incontinent, fierce, despisers of those that are good,

2Ti 3:4 traitors, heady, highminded, lovers of pleasures more than lovers of God;

2Ti 3:5 Having a form of godliness, but denying the power thereof: from such turn away.
2Ti 3:6 for of this sort are they which creep into houses, and lead captive silly women laden with sins, led away with divers lusts,
2Ti 3:7 Ever learning, and never able to come to the knowledge of the truth.

Our progeny, children and legacy are the fruit of our decisions, our own tree of good and evil. Curiously, millions of lives do not produce multitudes of expressions but repeat history and conform to codes, rules and behaviors that are categorized and studied.

Gen 5:3 And Adam lived an hundred and thirty years, and begat [a son] in his own likeness, after his image; and called his name Seth:

At the very beginning apart from God's garden proceed Adam and Eve. Human experience will now plumb God/no God living in a world apart from the Spirit of God. Our life consists of choices. Energy flows to areas of less energy just as the easy choice tests our beliefs. Commonly, people remark that a child resembles the father or mother and here the bible recognizes physical humanity's hope for their future. Apart from parental hopes however, children follow decisions of their own. Each birth initiates life that is more than simply a physical gene pool. Who we are is framed by but is not merely physical lineage. The mind of this world is to affix all to the physical, rejecting biblical insistence of the spiritual. Genesis relates that Cain is born then Abel but Cain lost his heritage when he killed his brother. Genesis then relates that Seth is born and replaces Abel. Seth is the third son born to Adam and Eve. Some passage of time and births occur without notice. There are others with whom Cain interacts without explanation of where they came from. In the first chapter man is created male and female on the sixth day.

Gen 1:27 So God created man in His [own] image, in the image of God created He him; male and female created He them.

Jhn 1:33 And I knew him not: but he that sent me to baptize with water, the same said unto me, Upon whom thou shalt see the Spirit descending, and remaining on him, the same is he which baptizeth with the Holy Ghost.

Jhn 7:39 (But this spake he of the Spirit, which they that believe on him should receive: for the Holy Ghost was not yet [given]; because that Jesus was not yet glorified.)

God rests on the seventh day. The bible then in the second chapter, adds details to the first chapter overview. Water and care for the plants are noted, followed by man's creation from the dust, God plants a garden eastward in Eden, the man is placed there, trees, rivers, and lands are described, then again scripture mentions that God put the man in the Garden, then comes the warning not to partake of the tree whereby comes the knowledge of good and evil, then God will make a companion for the lonely man, now the man is Adam and he names all living creatures, and then the next human is created. The verse following Genesis 2:23 where the woman is created for example, is an incongruent chronological sequence when referring to parents.

Gen 2:24 Therefore shall a man leave his father and his mother, and shall cleave unto his wife: and they shall be one flesh.

This declaration at the time the first woman is created establishes the terms of male, female relations. The first time manner of conduct must be decided. Adam proclaims the condition of marriage and is somewhat prophetic since the first human is created from the dust and the second human is newly arrived from a kind of cloning; there is no "Adam" father or mother. Cloning at the very beginning of humanity also

91

presages science centuries later. Before sin Adam's thoughts align with God.

Gen 2:7 And the LORD God formed man [of] the dust of the ground, and breathed into his nostrils the breath of life; and man became a living soul.
Gen 2:22 and the rib, which the LORD God had taken from man, made He a woman, and brought her unto the man.
Gen 2:23 And Adam said, this [is] now bone of my bones, and flesh of my flesh: she shall be called Woman, because she was taken out of Man.
Mat 19:6 Wherefore they are no more twain, but one flesh. What therefore God hath joined together, let not man put asunder.

Which are You?

Not until chapter 5 in the bloodline of Seth is the birth of daughters regularly noted. An accounting of a number of births would distract from what is to be known. Details are related after an event occurs that reveals an example or condition proving truth.   Right after Cain is pronounced a pariah, he is with his wife. Both his and Seth's children are accompanied by wives and all interact with others. If the book of Genesis is figurative there would be no need to trace personal names until the event of consequence occurs. Real people are responsible for notable acts. In the first 4 chapters all the wives and others are not named neither are the incidents of their births described. Births bring humans into the world but this knowledge is a natural condition without need of explanation and definitely would dilute presentation of the intended message. Entry into our world requires a mother. Common to every one of us, birth is of absolute necessity for humanity.   Mothers are this world's exclusive condition for existence. Thank God for loving and tender mothers.

The intended message is not diluted to distraction with extraneous details. All names and life spans are literal otherwise pronouns would effectively convey the concept clean of influence imparted with an identified character. The whole biblical revelation of the creation of human being is factual presentation concerning the participants including individual names. The book of life referred to almost exclusively in the last book of the bible is a record of names among other details. The book of life is also another indication of the precision of names with, and evidence that every person is known to God. Each person in the entirety of human existence is remarkable, is known. The life of each person is noted and has consequence. We are relevant, we creatures of God for his purpose. God has spoken and will require results of each life for the consequences that affect His creation. Every person will give back to God what they have done with their lease, their contract of life. Human being is not animal like reaction to the environment. Pray that you have somewhat to give back.

Luk 17:9 Doth he thank that servant because he did the things that were commanded him? I trow not.
Luk 17:10 So likewise ye, when ye shall have done all those things which are commanded you, say, We are unprofitable servants: we have done that which was our duty to do.
Mat 12:36 But I say unto you, That every idle word that men shall speak, they shall give account thereof in the day of judgment.
Mat 12:37 For by thy words thou shalt be justified, and by thy words thou shalt be condemned.
Mat 25:29 For unto every one that hath shall be given, and he shall have abundance: but from him that hath not shall be taken away even that which he hath.
Mat 25:30 And cast ye the unprofitable servant into outer darkness: there shall be weeping and gnashing of teeth.

Mat 25:31 When the Son of man shall come in his glory, and all the holy angels with him, then shall he sit upon the throne of his glory:

Mat 25:32 And before him shall be gathered all nations: and he shall separate them one from another, as a shepherd divideth [his] sheep from the goats:

Rom 14:12   So then every one of us shall give account of himself to God.

1Pe 4:3 For the time past of [our] life may suffice us to have wrought the will of the Gentiles, when we walked in lasciviousness, lusts, excess of wine, revellings, banquetings, and abominable idolatries:

1Pe 4:4   Wherein they think it strange that ye run not with [them] to the same excess of riot, speaking evil of [you]:

1Pe 4:5 Who shall give account to him that is ready to judge the quick and the dead.

1Pe 4:6 For for this cause was the gospel preached also to them that are dead, that they might be judged according to men in the flesh, but live according to God in the spirit.

1Pe 4:7 But the end of all things is at hand: be ye therefore sober, and watch unto prayer.

1Pe 4:8 And above all things have fervent charity among yourselves: for charity shall cover the multitude of sins.

Rev 4:10 The four and twenty elders fall down before him that sat on the throne, and worship him that liveth for ever and ever, and cast their crowns before the throne, saying,

Rev 4:11 Thou art worthy, O Lord, to receive glory and honour and power: for thou hast created all things, and for thy pleasure they are and were created.

Observation of the family tree of Cain ends after noting another man is slain by the 5th generation son of Cain, Lamech. At this end point of the mention of Cain's line of progeny more detail is conveyed. Here is the first instance of more than one wife. Here for the first time excepting Eve, wives have names. There are 3 sons born to Lamech and the first mention of the birth of a daughter. The occupations of the sons are listed, father of such that live in tents and herd cattle, father of all such that handle pipe and organ and, an instructor of every artificer in brass and iron. None are involved with farming. Lamech is a murderer in the likeness of his forefather. The lineage of Cain is recognized until the "whom" that is foremost in their worldview and lineage expresses the fruit of such a mind. The course of this lineage has tipped too far into consumption; creation from this mindset will conform to the behavior that evicted the one who was once the son of the morning. Fruits from this condition of being corrupt, there is no mind for God.

Gen 4:23 And Lamech said unto his wives, Adah and Zillah, Hear my voice; ye wives of Lamech, hearken unto my speech: for I have slain a man to my wounding, and a young man to my hurt.
Gen 4:24 If Cain shall be avenged sevenfold, truly Lamech seventy and sevenfold.

Pride and desire are come to fruition just as the covering cherub was cast out of the mountain of God and unrestrained excess was washed away, was eliminated through the cleansing flood at Noah. Sin is resilient, surviving dethronement, absolutions, purges and washings. This behavior is not a condition of natural selection that relieves excess. Sin is a terminal condition, the destructive behavior that refutes evolution inevitably progressing to cessation of the species. Unaddressed, sin succeeds to extinction. Death and birth forestall the completion of sin. Awareness is the component of good and evil, singular and exclusive to human being in this world.

Notable Quality

Gen 4:26 and to Seth, to him also there was born a son; and he called his name Enos: then began men to call upon the name of the LORD.
Gen 5:22 and Enoch walked with God after he begat Methuselah three hundred years, and begat sons and daughters:

Genesis notes that Enoch, 5th generation in Seth's bloodline, walked with God.
Adam's lineage is recognized through Seth who heeds God to avoid sin and remains obedient to His will. Robust humans loosed in a lush world did not give reign to lust. Apart from a final specific revelation of the manner of Cain's bloodline, there is scarce mention of anything of the pre flood world except for the line of Seth. Early human being is sin riddled excess, lacking dignity of spirit to become a tragedy fit only to be erased. Pride is haughty, is persistent, competitive, combative, murderous, truly without conscience for the lives of anyone else. Pride does not readily accept the shameful behavior of early humans. Biblical revelation is the tonic for all manner of rationalization, imagination or excuse constructed to account for human behavior and the course of creation. Humans had no mind for their loving creator.

Completely lost to excess, humans became a festering presence oblivious, demeaning the creation of God. Angry and anguished God eliminated these beings that did not comprehend the reality of life expressing beauty, dignity, encouragement, fulfillment, grace, purpose, truth actively effecting creation in the image of God. Noah is the exception who heeds the will of God thereby escaping the judgment of the flood.

Gen 6:5 and GOD saw that the wickedness of man [was] great in the earth, and [that] every imagination of the thoughts of his heart [was] only evil continually.
Gen 6:6 and it repented the LORD that he had made man on the earth, and it grieved him at his heart.
Gen 6:7 and the LORD said, I will destroy man whom I have created from the face of the earth; both man, and beast, and the creeping thing, and the fowls of the air; for it repenteth me that I have made them.
Gen 7:21 and all flesh died that moved upon the earth, both of fowl, and of cattle, and of beast, and of every creeping thing that creepeth upon the earth, and every man:
Gen 7:22 All in whose nostrils [was] the breath of life, of all that [was] in the dry [land], died.
Gen 7:23 and every living substance was destroyed which was upon the face of the ground, both man, and cattle, and the creeping things, and the fowl of the heaven; and they were destroyed from the earth: and Noah only remained [alive], and they that [were] with him in the ark.

Chapter 6
Of Their Own

Quickening the dead and calling that which is not as though it is describes supernatural behavior. Our mind in this life is so contrary to spiritual behavior, it can only be noted as strident contrast or "enmity" to God. Humans developed into an image and all the sons and daughters conform to the likeness yet produce fruit of their own and exhibit a variety of behaviors due to the knowledge of good and evil. Deception, jealousy, lust, pride, anger and hatred contrast God-like behavior. These behaviors are destructive; they do not create. Human dignity is lost through these practices that have blighted human being. Creation has been entangled and thwarted in this "human" problem contrary to the Word of God. When the awareness of "who" was enhanced by the knowledge of good and evil humans left the will of God for their own pursuits. Self promotion prefers apart from the place or rights of others. Glorified self discounts the will of God and rationalizes the denial of God.

Rom 4:17 (As it is written, I have made thee a father of many nations,) before him whom he believed, [even] God, who quickeneth the dead, and calleth those things which be not as though they were.
1Pe 4:6 For this cause was the gospel preached also to them that are dead, that they might be judged according to men in the flesh, but live according to God in the spirit.
1Pe 4:17 For the time [is come] that judgment must begin at the house of God: and if [it] first [begin] at us, what shall the end [be] of them that obey not the gospel of God?
1Pe 4:18 And if the righteous scarcely be saved, where shall the ungodly and the sinner appear?

1Pe 4:19 Wherefore let them that suffer according to the will of God commit the keeping of their souls [to him] in well doing, as unto a faithful Creator.

Jhn 4:23 But the hour cometh, and now is, when the true worshippers shall worship the Father in spirit and in truth: for the Father seeketh such to worship him.

Jhn 4:24 God [is] a Spirit: and they that worship him must worship [him] in spirit and in truth.

Rom 8:7 Because the carnal mind [is] enmity against God: for it is not subject to the law of God, neither indeed can be.

Pro 16:25 There is a way that seemeth right unto a man, but the end thereof [are] the ways of death.

1Cr 10:11 Now all these things happened unto them for ensamples: and they are written for our admonition, upon whom the ends of the world are come.

This world is very far indeed from God's creation, His plan. Humans must reorder their thoughts, their life experience to consider God and others question whether there is God at all. Human pride, humanism increases the separation from God. It is deemed intelligence and sophistication that denies the biblical creation account. Within humanity are varieties of being that desire, that war with their own siblings conforming to our creator's warning. War, the fruit of envy, esteem, lust, pride or hate is with us today just as Cain slew Abel. Cain's prideful, selfish behavior was a first example of others historic or current. Thought will be effected, it will be realized.

Phl 4:8 Finally, brethren, whatsoever things are true, whatsoever things [are] honest, whatsoever things [are] just, whatsoever things [are] pure, whatsoever things [are] lovely, whatsoever things [are] of good report; if [there be] any virtue, and if [there be] any praise, think on these things.

Phl 4:9 Those things, which ye have both learned, and received, and heard, and seen in me, do: and the God of peace shall be with you.

The original human sin produced fruit according to choices that reveal the heart. A scriptural example of this condition is described as, "the fruit tree yielding fruit after his kind, whose seed [is] in itself, upon the earth ". The statement, "whose seed is in itself", does convey accountability for our decisions and this type exists "upon the earth". We are responsible for our behavior not some other agent or agency. Sin seeks excuse. Genesis, the beginning, describes this condition through 2 bloodlines, the murdering son Cain and the replacement son Seth. Cain's bloodline follows after he extracts a condition of safety for his life on the earth, thus revealing his mind. He ascribes his behavior to others by indicating his fear of being slain. The potential for additional murder is with Cain even after he is assured of his safety. His thought is focused on the physical and his conduct on earth. Cain's manner is destructive to God's creation not merely due to the need for others now to defend against murder but due to his focus apart from his creator. Cain's mind is to acquire and grow for himself preempting the existence of others. This behavior reveals that Cain has no regard for God's advice.

Gen 4:6 and the LORD said unto Cain, Why art thou wroth? And why is thy countenance fallen?
Gen 4:7 If thou doest well, shalt thou not be accepted? And if thou doest not well, sin lieth at the door. And unto thee [shall be] his desire, and thou shalt rule over him.

Those who sin, Adam and Eve, Cain and the rest of us will continue in that behavior. The motive for sin will exercise the sinful behavior as similar conditions that prompted the first sin arise. The sinful behavior is then the manner of conduct and will induce other sins. The first sin of Adam and Eve was an offense to God's love. Sin is in us and continues to corrupt.

100

Corruption and disintegration do not build but are components of reduction or death. Reality is not spontaneous occurrence of intelligence destined to step beyond human that also just appeared and is different than any other existing life. Evolution cannot produce human or higher, superhuman creatures. If considered from a scientific perspective, evolution does not progress to supernatural states of existence due to its undergirding tenet. Natural selection purportedly produces the optimum organism for the physical environment. That physical environment is spiritless. Witness the animals. We are expected to believe that humans alone acquired this awareness and not conversely, why we exclusively, are so evolved. Science is not contrary to the biblical account. Science does err though by each degree of separation from human personality and cultural expression and is wholly lost in matters of spirit. Scripture relates that the natural man cannot know the things of the spirit. Evolution can never admit that this is a created hierarchy. We are to believe that humans just coalesced within this fragile globe. Humans apart from any other animal are the only occurrence of a type. This world is too small to produce the human being. Our being is impossible as a sterile manikin; a world without smiles does not mirror human character. There is more to human being than a confluence of elements. The contest between God or evolution delivers us to the question that does determine our behavior, who are we?

The knowledge of self affects the individual and the whole race. Self is knowledge of good and evil. Consider for instance, pride. Pride is harmful in the disdain of others. Pride has harmed every person who has walked this earth. Pride's harm is multitudinous but think on the human mentality. Pride cannot accept God. Some, who reject evolutionary transition from slime to humanity theory, propose the transition to human resulted instead from alien manipulation of the animal. Aliens are only better than humans due to the advanced state of their science. Human pride is vindicated because the human race can attain that level of science. This concept still fails to account for that uncomfortable leap from animal to a being with spiritual awareness.

Rom 8:5 For they that are after the flesh do mind the things of the flesh; but they that are after the Spirit the things of the Spirit.
Mar 10:15 Verily I say unto you, Whosoever shall not receive the kingdom of God as a little child, he shall not enter therein.
Luk 18:17 Verily I say unto you, Whosoever shall not receive the kingdom of God as a little child shall in no wise enter therein.

Since our experience is primarily physical it is surprising that we acknowledge a spiritual existence. Spiritual allusions and beliefs occur in all cultures. This is a peculiar, difficult behavior that is incongruent within the physical world.

1Cr 2:11 For what man knoweth the things of a man, save the spirit of man which is in him? even so the things of God knoweth no man, but the Spirit of God.
1Cr 2:12 Now we have received, not the spirit of the world, but the spirit which is of God; that we might know the things that are freely given to us of God.
1Cr 2:13 Which things also we speak, not in the words which man's wisdom teacheth, but which the Holy Ghost teacheth; comparing spiritual things with spiritual.
1Cr 2:14 But the natural man receiveth not the things of the Spirit of God: for they are foolishness unto him: neither can he know [them], because they are spiritually discerned.

We are the exception that is not made by evolution but created in the image of God; created and fallen. Sinful human nature, the flesh, prevails as overtly evidenced in Genesis. Without a redeemer to deliver us from the natural manner of sinners we are terminal. There is no internal change agent or method for those whose manner is sin to change that course. Behavior creates a new being, a new mind that interacts among human populations wholly participating in the current reality. We are entrapped in error. Redemption requires a work of God. God is the true creator.

Jhn 8:34 Jesus answered them, Verily, verily, I say unto you, Whosoever committeth sin is the servant of sin.
Rom 7:18 For I know that in me (that is, in my flesh,) dwelleth no good thing: for to will is present with me; but [how] to perform that which is good I find not.
Rom 7:24 O wretched man that I am! who shall deliver me from the body of this death?

Seth's bloodline is recognized with the observation that men began to call upon the name of the Lord. This acknowledgement of God continues through to the judgment at Noah. Noah reveals his heart in devoting all his effort to building the Ark and thereby disdaining the world.

Gen 6:8 but Noah found grace in the eyes of the LORD.
Gen 6:22 Thus did Noah; according to all that God commanded him, so did he.
Gen 7:1 and the LORD said unto Noah, Come thou and all thy house into the ark; for thee have I seen righteous before me in this generation.
Gen 7:5 and Noah did according unto all that the LORD commanded him.

Who are Unaware

The omission of anyone outside of Noah's family with this work of God indicts humanity, those who are dead. Focus apart from God is now the human condition. Sin has overwhelmed all. There were no other arks built. Pre flood people were wholly preoccupied within the affairs of their lives. There was no regard for their creator from sunrise to sunset. Noah was the exception at the fringe and likely discounted at least as unsophisticated more likely as a fool who expended his wealth on this massive yet seemingly irrelevant construction. That community could not miss what he was doing and did not believe his preaching. The pre flood world was surprised with destruction that surely has parallels for those consumed with the cares of this life, who will follow their ancestors into the grave, to death.

Luk 21:34 And take heed to yourselves, lest at any time your hearts be overcharged with surfeiting, and drunkenness, and cares of this life, and [so] that day come upon you unawares.
Luk 21:35 For as a snare shall it come on all them that dwell on the face of the whole earth.
Luk 21:36 Watch ye therefore, and pray always, that ye may be accounted worthy to escape all these things that shall come to pass, and to stand before the Son of man.
Mat 13:13 Therefore speak I to them in parables: because they seeing see not; and hearing they hear not, neither do they understand.
Mat 13:14 And in them is fulfilled the prophecy of Esaias, which saith, By hearing ye shall hear, and shall not understand; and seeing ye shall see, and shall not perceive:
Mat 13:15 For this people's heart is waxed gross, and [their] ears are dull of hearing, and their eyes they have closed; lest at any time they should see with [their] eyes, and hear with [their] ears, and should understand with [their] heart, and should be converted, and I should heal them.
Mat 13:16 But blessed [are] your eyes, for they see: and your ears, for they hear.

Gen 6:1 and it came to pass, when men began to multiply on the face of the earth, and daughters were born unto them,

Gen 6:2 that the sons of God saw the daughters of men that they [were] fair; and they took them wives of all which they chose.

Gen 6:3 and the LORD said, My spirit shall not always strive with man, for that he also [is] flesh: yet his days shall be an hundred and twenty years.

Gen 6:4 There were giants in the earth in those days; and also after that, when the sons of God came in unto the daughters of men, and they bare [children] to them, the same [became] mighty men which [were] of old, men of renown.

Gen 6:5 and GOD saw that the wickedness of man [was] great in the earth, and [that] every imagination of the thoughts of his heart [was] only evil continually.

Gen 6:6 and it repented the LORD that he had made man on the earth, and it grieved him at his heart.

Gal 5:19 Now the works of the flesh are manifest, which are [these]; Adultery, fornication, uncleanness, lasciviousness,

Gal 5:20 Idolatry, witchcraft, hatred, variance, emulations, wrath, strife, seditions, heresies,

Gal 5:21 Envyings, murders, drunkenness, revellings, and such like: of the which I tell you before, as I have also told [you] in time past, that they which do such things shall not inherit the kingdom of God.

2Pe 2:4 For if God spared not the angels that sinned, but cast [them] down to hell, and delivered [them] into chains of darkness, to be reserved unto judgment;

2Pe 2:5 And spared not the old world, but saved Noah the eighth [person], a preacher of righteousness, bringing in the flood upon the world of the ungodly;

2Pe 2:6 And turning the cities of Sodom and Gomorrha into ashes condemned [them] with an overthrow, making [them] an ensample unto those that after should live ungodly;

2Pe 2:7 And delivered just Lot, vexed with the filthy conversation of the wicked:

2Pe 2:8 (For that righteous man dwelling among them, in seeing and hearing, vexed [his] righteous soul from day to day with [their] unlawful deeds;)

2Pe 2:9 The Lord knoweth how to deliver the godly out of temptations, and to reserve the unjust unto the day of judgment to be punished:

2Pe 2:10 But chiefly them that walk after the flesh in the lust of uncleanness, and despise government. Presumptuous [are they], selfwilled, they are not afraid to speak evil of dignities.

2Pe 2:11 Whereas angels, which are greater in power and might, bring not railing accusation against them before the Lord.

2Pe 2:12 But these, as natural brute beasts, made to be taken and destroyed, speak evil of the things that they understand not; and shall utterly perish in their own corruption;

2Pe 2:13 And shall receive the reward of unrighteousness, [as] they that count it pleasure to riot in the day time. Spots [they are] and blemishes, sporting themselves with their own deceivings while they feast with you;

2Pe 2:14 Having eyes full of adultery, and that cannot cease from sin; beguiling unstable souls: an heart they have exercised with covetous practices; cursed children:

Gen 6:7 and the LORD said, I will destroy man whom I have created from the face of the earth; both man, and beast, and the creeping thing, and the fowls of the air; for it repenteth me that I have made them.

Gen 8:21 and the LORD smelled a sweet savour; and the LORD said in his heart, I will not again curse the ground any more for man's sake; for the imagination of man's heart [is] evil from his youth; neither will I again smite any more every thing living, as I have done.

Gen 8:22 While the earth remaineth, seedtime and harvest, and cold and heat, and summer and winter, and day and night shall not cease.

Gen 9:11 and I will establish my covenant with you; neither shall all flesh be cut off any more by the waters of a flood; neither shall there any more be a flood to destroy the earth.

Sin wholly offends God. It grieves God beyond our imagination. It is God who has and does suffer with the corruption, the contradiction of sin that afflicts His creation.

Sin is terrible tragedy; alas, what might have been is lost!

1Jo 2:16 For all that [is] in the world, the lust of the flesh, and the lust of the eyes, and the pride of life, is not of the Father, but is of the world.

1Cr 15:50 Now this I say, brethren, that flesh and blood cannot inherit the kingdom of God; neither doth corruption inherit incorruption.

Mat 26:41 Watch and pray, that ye enter not into temptation: the spirit indeed [is] willing, but the flesh [is] weak. Also Mark 14:38

Rom 6:19 I speak after the manner of men because of the infirmity of your flesh: for as ye have yielded your members servants to uncleanness and to iniquity unto iniquity; even so now yield your members servants to righteousness unto holiness.

Mal 3:7 Even from the days of your fathers ye are gone away from mine ordinances, and have not kept [them]. Return unto me, and I will return unto you, saith the LORD of hosts. But ye said, Wherein shall we return?

1Jo 1:9 If we confess our sins, he is faithful and just to forgive us [our] sins, and to cleanse us from all unrighteousness.

Psa 103:8 The LORD [is] merciful and gracious, slow to anger, and plenteous in mercy.

Psa 103:9 He will not always chide: neither will he keep [his anger] for ever.

Psa 103:10 He hath not dealt with us after our sins; nor rewarded us according to our iniquities.

Psa 103:11 For as the heaven is high above the earth, [so] great is his mercy toward them that fear him.

Psa 103:12 As far as the east is from the west, [so] far hath he removed our transgressions from us.

Psa 103:13 Like as a father pitieth [his] children, [so] the LORD pitieth them that fear him.

Psa 103:14 For he knoweth our frame; he remembereth that we [are] dust.

Psa 103:15 [As for] man, his days [are] as grass: as a flower of the field, so he flourisheth.

Psa 103:16 For the wind passeth over it, and it is gone; and the place thereof shall know it no more.

Psa 103:17 But the mercy of the LORD [is] from everlasting to everlasting upon them that fear him, and his righteousness unto children's children;

1Cr 15:43 It is sown in dishonour; it is raised in glory: it is sown in weakness; it is raised in power:

Gal 5:16 [This] I say then, Walk in the Spirit, and ye shall not fulfill the lust of the flesh.

Gal 5:17 For the flesh lusteth against the Spirit, and the Spirit against the flesh: and these are contrary the one to the other: so that ye cannot do the things that ye would.

In this era of change it is especially critical to make certain God's purpose is paramount. The creator is perfect, the creation wanes proportional to separation from the source. The lesser separation was a physical loss. The mind focused elsewhere than participation with God departs from the creator, from creation into dissolution. Our separation from God is a spiritual cleavage. Our heart, our comportment and interests that were to continue creation turned rather to consumption. God's Holy Spirit was severed at Adam and Eve's sin. Consider how harsh and even absurd the subject of spirit and spiritual creation appears to flesh and blood but yet does not the word say,

Jhn 4:24 God [is] a Spirit: and they that worship him must worship [him] in spirit and in truth."
Mat 7:13 Enter ye in at the strait gate: for wide [is] the gate, and broad [is] the way, that leadeth to destruction, and many there be which go in thereat:
Mat 7:14 Because strait [is] the gate, and narrow [is] the way, which leadeth unto life, and few there be that find it.
Rev 2:7 He that hath an ear, let him hear what the Spirit saith unto the churches; To him that overcometh will I give to eat of the tree of life, which is in the midst of the paradise of God.
Rev 22:2 In the midst of the street of it, and on either side of the river, [was there] the tree of life, which bare twelve [manner of] fruits, [and] yielded her fruit every month: and the leaves of the tree [were] for the healing of the nations.
Rev 22:14 Blessed [are] they that do his commandments, that they may have right to the tree of life, and may enter in through the gates into the city.

Jam 1:11 For the sun is no sooner risen with a burning heat, but it withereth the grass, and the flower thereof falleth, and the grace of the fashion of it perisheth: so also shall the rich man fade away in his ways.

Jam 1:12 Blessed [is] the man that endureth temptation: for when he is tried, he shall receive the crown of life, which the Lord hath promised to them that love him.

Jam 1:13 Let no man say when he is tempted, I am tempted of God: for God cannot be tempted with evil, neither tempteth he any man:

Jam 1:14 But every man is tempted, when he is drawn away of his own lust, and enticed.

Jam 1:15 Then when lust hath conceived, it bringeth forth sin: and sin, when it is finished, bringeth forth death.

Jam 1:16 Do not err, my beloved brethren.

Jam 1:17 Every good gift and every perfect gift is from above, and cometh down from the Father of lights, with whom is no variableness, neither shadow of turning.

Jam 1:18 Of his own will begat he us with the word of truth, that we should be a kind of firstfruits of his creatures.

Jam 1:19 Wherefore, my beloved brethren, let every man be swift to hear, slow to speak, slow to wrath:

Jam 1:20 For the wrath of man worketh not the righteousness of God.

Rom 6:23 For the wages of sin [is] death; but the gift of God [is] eternal life through Jesus Christ our Lord.

It is Disobedience

Humans did not fall like the anointed cherub when accumulation of iniquity was found in them; it was by a specific act. Adam and Eve were deceived. Genesis only describes an instance of desire not an accumulation of willfulness, but relates more of a new desire that discounts the perfect truth of God. Surely if an excuse could suffice or absolve disobedience, this is the perfect setting. In this instance Genesis reveals that the insufferable offense of sin cannot be neglected. Sin is a fertile seed that is more than interruption it corrupts, it is destruction not creation; it is not the image of God. Here at the very beginning Adam and Eve were ashamed to admit that they themselves had actually begun to corrupt God's creation.

Gen 3:12 And the man said, The woman whom thou gavest [to be] with me, she gave me of the tree, and I did eat.
Gen 3:13 And the LORD God said unto the woman, What [is] this [that] thou hast done? And the woman said, The serpent beguiled me, and I did eat.

After responsibility is recognized we seek to rationalize the offense as merely a slip up. It is our manner. We do not care to see our own guilt so we hide the truth in denial.   Our self esteem is tainted by offensive behavior and so we attempt to disown our role. Our preferred and cultivated self assessments discourage repentance and lead us away from the will of God. Assigning responsibility for our choices to anyone or thing rejects the forgiveness, the lovingkindness of God and forestalls His kingdom for our lives and the earth. Choice produces fruit. Prideful and selfish choices have obstructed the work of God. Choice is gifted to us; therefore our decisions or obedience will not be commanded.

Mat 13:57 And they were offended in him. But Jesus said unto them, A prophet is not without honour, save in his own country, and in his own house.
Mat 13:58 And he did not many mighty works there because of their unbelief.

What we do is who and what we are. The first man and woman doubted God, chose the fruit of knowledge and found death in disobedience. There remains a hope of everlasting life but corruption cannot inherit incorruption. Who we are, our

111

image is not in the image of God because of our personal choices, our fruit. Our choices, our will can partake of the Kingdom of God or choose desire apart from God's will that eventually succumbs to the degradation and corruption Satan has chosen.

2Ti 1:1 Paul, an apostle of Jesus Christ by the will of God, according to the promise of life which is in Christ Jesus,

Every single person is accountable apart from some membership or other blanket absolution; choice is given and judged by God. Each, every human will review their personal life before God. Sinful behavior can be overcome as evidenced by the patience of God with sinners.   God is the true creator Who does redeem those who repent and seek His will. God forgives anytime, every time we ask. God provides redemption for those who accept His salvation but at some time everyone will face judgment.   A lifetime is a gift that can be tragic or glorious.

Gal 5:17 For the flesh lusteth against the Spirit, and the Spirit against the flesh: and these are contrary the one to the other: so that ye cannot do the things that ye would.
Jam 1:14 But every man is tempted, when he is drawn away of his own lust, and enticed.
Jam 1:15 Then when lust hath conceived, it bringeth forth sin: and sin, when it is finished, bringeth forth death.
Jam 4:5 Do ye think that the scripture saith in vain, The spirit that dwelleth in us lusteth to envy?
Pro 5:21 For the ways of man [are] before the eyes of the LORD, and he pondereth all his goings.
Pro 5:22 His own iniquities shall take the wicked himself, and he shall be holden with the cords of his sins.

Pro 5:23 He shall die without instruction; and in the greatness of his folly he shall go astray.

Isa 57:15 For thus saith the high and lofty One that inhabiteth eternity, whose name [is] Holy; I dwell in the high and holy [place], with him also [that is] of a contrite and humble spirit, to revive the spirit of the humble, and to revive the heart of the contrite ones.

Isa 57:16 For I will not contend for ever, neither will I be always wroth: for the spirit should fail before me, and the souls [which] I have made.

Isa 57:17 For the iniquity of his covetousness was I wroth, and smote him: I hid me, and was wroth, and he went on frowardly in the way of his heart.

Isa 57:18 I have seen his ways, and will heal him: I will lead him also, and restore comforts unto him and to his mourners.

Isa 57:19 I create the fruit of the lips; Peace, peace to [him that is] far off, and to [him that is] near, saith the LORD; and I will heal him.

Isa 57:20 But the wicked [are] like the troubled sea, when it cannot rest, whose waters cast up mire and dirt.

Isa 57:21 [There is] no peace, saith my God, to the wicked.

Psa 51:2 Wash me throughly from mine iniquity, and cleanse me from my sin.

Psa 51:3 For I acknowledge my transgressions: and my sin [is] ever before me.

Psa 51:4 Against thee, thee only, have I sinned, and done [this] evil in thy sight: that thou mightest be justified when thou speakest, [and] be clear when thou judgest.

Psa 51:5 Behold, I was shapen in iniquity; and in sin did my mother conceive me.

Psa 51:6 Behold, thou desirest truth in the inward parts: and in the hidden [part] thou shalt make me to know wisdom.

Psa 51:7 Purge me with hyssop, and I shall be clean: wash me, and I shall be whiter than snow.
Psa 51:8 Make me to hear joy and gladness; [that] the bones [which] thou hast broken may rejoice.
Psa 51:9 Hide thy face from my sins, and blot out all mine iniquities.
Psa 51:10 Create in me a clean heart, O God; and renew a right spirit within me.
Psa 51:11 Cast me not away from thy presence; and take not thy holy spirit from me.
Psa 51:12 Restore unto me the joy of thy salvation; and uphold me [with thy] free spirit.
Psa 51:13 [Then] will I teach transgressors thy ways; and sinners shall be converted unto thee.
Psa 51:14 Deliver me from bloodguiltiness, O God, thou God of my salvation: [and] my tongue shall sing aloud of thy righteousness.
Psa 51:15 O Lord, open thou my lips; and my mouth shall shew forth thy praise.
Psa 51:16 For thou desirest not sacrifice; else would I give [it]: thou delightest not in burnt offering.
Psa 51:17 The sacrifices of God [are] a broken spirit: a broken and a contrite heart, O God, thou wilt not despise.

Some have said that we were patterned after Jesus' physical body since we were predestined, conformed to the image of His Son. Is the physical body really the image of God? Is God both male and female then as others have said or is sex merely a physical condition of this world? In Genesis 5:2 male and female are noted as, "Adam" and "Mankind". Creation is the purpose for each life. Choice is opportunity that delivers or discounts the image of God. In the bungling, embarrassments and dirt of our common lives, the wisdom of God accomplishes the profound act of creation in His Image.

1Cr 1:25 Because the foolishness of God is wiser than men; and the weakness of God is stronger than men.

1Cr 1:26 For ye see your calling, brethren, how that not many wise men after the flesh, not many mighty, not many noble, [are called]:

1Cr 1:27 But God hath chosen the foolish things of the world to confound the wise; and God hath chosen the weak things of the world to confound the things which are mighty;

1Cr 1:28 And base things of the world, and things which are despised, hath God chosen, [yea], and things which are not, to bring to nought things that are:

1Cr 1:29 That no flesh should glory in his presence.

1Cr 1:30 But of him are ye in Christ Jesus, who of God is made unto us wisdom, and righteousness, and sanctification, and redemption:

1Cr 1:31 That, according as it is written, He that glorieth, let him glory in the Lord.

Mat 11:29 Take my yoke upon you, and learn of me; for I am meek and lowly in heart: and ye shall find rest unto your souls.

Mat 5:5 Blessed [are] the meek: for they shall inherit the earth.

Zep 2:3 Seek ye the LORD, all ye meek of the earth, which have wrought his judgment; seek righteousness, seek meekness: it may be ye shall be hid in the day of the LORD'S anger.

1Cr 15:42 So also [is] the resurrection of the dead. It is sown in corruption; it is raised in incorruption:

1Cr 15:43 It is sown in dishonour; it is raised in glory: it is sown in weakness; it is raised in power:

1Cr 15:44 It is sown a natural body; it is raised a spiritual body. There is a natural body, and there is a spiritual body.

1Cr 15:45 And so it is written, The first man Adam was made a living soul; the last Adam [was made] a quickening spirit.

1Cr 15:46 Howbeit that [was] not first which is spiritual, but that which is natural; and afterward that which is spiritual.

1Cr 15:47 The first man [is] of the earth, earthy: the second man [is] the Lord from heaven.

1Cr 15:48 As [is] the earthy, such [are] they also that are earthy: and as [is] the heavenly, such [are] they also that are heavenly.

1Cr 15:49 And as we have borne the image of the earthy, we shall also bear the image of the heavenly.

1Cr 15:50 Now this I say, brethren, that flesh and blood cannot inherit the kingdom of God; neither doth corruption inherit incorruption.

Jhn 4:24 God [is] a Spirit: and they that worship him must worship [him] in spirit and in truth.

Jhn 3:31 He that cometh from above is above all: he that is of the earth is earthly, and speaketh of the earth: he that cometh from heaven is above all.

Act 7:49 Heaven [is] my throne, and earth [is] my footstool: what house will ye build me? saith the Lord: or what [is] the place of my rest?

Exd 33:19 And he said, I will make all my goodness pass before thee, and I will proclaim the name of the LORD before thee; and will be gracious to whom I will be gracious, and will shew mercy on whom I will shew mercy.

Exd 33:20 And he said, Thou canst not see my face: for there shall no man see me, and live.

Exd 33:21 And the LORD said, Behold, [there is] a place by me, and thou shalt stand upon a rock:

Exd 33:22 And it shall come to pass, while my glory passeth by, that I will put thee in a clift of the rock, and will cover thee with my hand while I pass by:

Exd 33:23 And I will take away mine hand, and thou shalt see my back parts: but my face shall not be seen.

Is That All There Is?

Today we are forsaking the image of God in our manner, our thoughts, in the conduct of our lives. The image of Satan rejects God. Corruption does not inherit incorruption. Our kind is not so successful as creators as we are consumers and corruptors. This world is too far from God's will. It is not remarkable that sin feels comfortable and finds excuse. It is the will of God that discomforts here. Each person decides for or against God daily making this a very personal choice. There is no limit to the explanations that discount God. Who and what are we? Human self- esteem and intentions are mocked by death. The irony of human existence is captured by the summary question, "Is that all there is?" Despair haunts the outcome of even the richest lives and all that are expended in consumption rather than building character and their spirit. Choices of physical considerations within our lives occur without a thought for the purpose, the will of God.

Luk 12:16 And he spake a parable unto them, saying, The ground of a certain rich man brought forth plentifully:
Luk 12:17 And he thought within himself, saying, What shall I do, because I have no room where to bestow my fruits?
Luk 12:18 And he said, This will I do: I will pull down my barns, and build greater; and there will I bestow all my fruits and my goods.
Luk 12:19 And I will say to my soul, Soul, thou hast much goods laid up for many years; take thine ease, eat, drink, [and] be merry.
Luk 12:20 But God said unto him, [Thou] fool, this night thy soul shall be required of thee: then whose shall those things be, which thou hast provided?
Luk 12:21 So [is] he that layeth up treasure for himself, and is not rich toward God.

Luk 12:22 And he said unto his disciples, Therefore I say unto you, Take no thought for your life, what ye shall eat; neither for the body, what ye shall put on.
Luk 12:23 The life is more than meat, and the body [is more] than raiment.
Rom 12:2 And be not conformed to this world: but be ye transformed by the renewing of your mind, that ye may prove what [is] that good, and acceptable, and perfect, will of God.
1Cr 7:31 And they that use this world, as not abusing [it]: for the fashion of this world passeth away.
1Jo 2:16 For all that [is] in the world, the lust of the flesh, and the lust of the eyes, and the pride of life, is not of the Father, but is of the world
Mat 16:26   For what is a man profited, if he shall gain the whole world, and lose his own soul? or what shall a man give in exchange for his soul?

Now the extremity that is to be like Jesus comes into focus. Are we made according to the physical body of Jesus?

Isa 53:2 For He shall grow up before Him as a tender plant, and as a root out of a dry ground: He hath no form nor comeliness; and when we shall see Him, [there is] no beauty that we should desire Him.
Rom 8:29 For whom He did foreknow, He also did predestinate [to be] conformed to the image of His Son, that He might be the firstborn among many brethren.
Jhn 6:38 For I came down from heaven, not to do mine own will, but the will of him that sent me.
Jhn 8:29 And he that sent me is with me: the Father hath not left me alone; for I do always those things that please him.
Gal 4:3 Even so we, when we were children, were in bondage under the elements of the world:

Gal 4:4 But when the fulness of the time was come, God sent forth his Son, made of a woman, made under the law,

Gal 4:5 To redeem them that were under the law, that we might receive the adoption of sons.

Gal 4:6 And because ye are sons, God hath sent forth the Spirit of his Son into your hearts, crying, Abba, Father.

Gal 4:7 Wherefore thou art no more a servant, but a son; and if a son, then an heir of God through Christ.

Eph 1:4 According as he hath chosen us in him before the foundation of the world, that we should be holy and without blame before him in love:

1Pe 1:20 Who verily was foreordained before the foundation of the world, but was manifest in these last times for you,

Or are we to be among those predestined to conform to the image of obedience that ultimately transforms flesh and death into the resurrection or transformation of/into the spiritual body that God has intended all along, the body that does not die?

Gal 4:6 And because ye are sons, God hath sent forth the Spirit of His Son into your hearts, crying, Abba, Father.

Psa 40:8 I delight to do thy will, O my God: yea, thy law [is] within my heart.

Psa 19:14 Let the words of my mouth, and the meditation of my heart, be acceptable in thy sight, O LORD, my strength, and my redeemer.

Rom 8:19 For the earnest expectation of the creature waiteth for the manifestation of the sons of God.

Rom 8:23 And not only [they], but ourselves also, which have the firstfruits of the Spirit, even we ourselves groan within ourselves, waiting for the adoption, [to wit], the redemption of our body.

Rom 13:11 And that, knowing the time, that now [it is] high time to awake out of sleep: for now [is] our salvation nearer than when we believed.
Rom 13:12 The night is far spent, the day is at hand: let us therefore cast off the works of darkness, and let us put on the armour of light.
Rom 13:13 Let us walk honestly, as in the day; not in rioting and drunkenness, not in chambering and wantonness, not in strife and envying.
Rom 13:14 But put ye on the Lord Jesus Christ, and make not provision for the flesh, to [fulfil] the lusts [thereof].
1Cr 15:34 Awake to righteousness, and sin not; for some have not the knowledge of God: I speak [this] to your shame.
Eph 5:14 Wherefore he saith, Awake thou that sleepest, and arise from the dead, and Christ shall give thee light.
1Ti 4:10 For therefore we both labour and suffer reproach, because we trust in the living God, who is the Saviour of all men, specially of those that believe.
1Pe 1:3 Blessed [be] the God and Father of our Lord Jesus Christ, which according to His abundant mercy hath begotten us again unto a lively hope by the resurrection of Jesus Christ from the dead,

Jesus would not be distracted. Jesus offended authority and was a disruption because of His single minded purpose, His entire focus, to do God's will. Clearly those who were chosen in Him before the foundation of the world were so identified because they have the opportunity to be holy and without blame in Him. Children of God in Him who are very different than the disobedient manner of the majority of human being. Jesus, "was foreordained before the foundation of the world, but was manifest in these last times" to recreate humans into the image and likeness of God. The identification of last times indicates the final act of the creation of human in the image of

120

God. The purpose and glory of God exists before the
foundation of this one world and times that accomplish
creation of human being in the image of God, the creation
process of man in the image of God. Jesus sacrificed Himself,
the will of God once at the end of the world. The end of the
world as perceived by the deathless without time, who are.
The end of the world and last times declare that there will be
no further changes. The plural times have continued through
to our lives for whosoever will repent, change and accept
Jesus.

Hbr 9:26 For then must he often have suffered since
the foundation of the world: but now once in the end
of the world hath he appeared to put away sin by the
sacrifice of himself.
2Cr 4:4 In whom the god of this world hath blinded
the minds of them which believe not, lest the light of
the glorious gospel of Christ, who is the image of God,
should shine unto them.
2Pe 3:3 Knowing this first, that there shall come in the
last days scoffers, walking after their own lusts,
2Pe 3:4 And saying, Where is the promise of his
coming? for since the fathers fell asleep, all things
continue as [they were] from the beginning of the
creation.
2Pe 3:5 For this they willingly are ignorant of, that by
the word of God the heavens were of old, and the
earth standing out of the water and in the water:
2Pe 3:6 Whereby the world that then was, being
overflowed with water, perished:
2Pe 3:7 But the heavens and the earth, which are
now, by the same word are kept in store, reserved
unto fire against the day of judgment and perdition of
ungodly men.
2Pe 3:8 But, beloved, be not ignorant of this one
thing, that one day [is] with the Lord as a thousand
years, and a thousand years as one day.

2Pe 3:9 The Lord is not slack concerning his promise, as some men count slackness; but is longsuffering to us-ward, not willing that any should perish, but that all should come to repentance.

2Pe 3:10 But the day of the Lord will come as a thief in the night; in the which the heavens shall pass away with a great noise, and the elements shall melt with fervent heat, the earth also and the works that are therein shall be burned up.

2Pe 3:11 [Seeing] then [that] all these things shall be dissolved, what manner [of persons] ought ye to be in [all] holy conversation and godliness,

2Pe 3:12 Looking for and hasting unto the coming of the day of God, wherein the heavens being on fire shall be dissolved, and the elements shall melt with fervent heat?

Luk 4:7 If thou therefore wilt worship me, all shall be thine.

Luk 4:8 and Jesus answered and said unto him, Get thee behind me, Satan: for it is written, Thou shalt worship the Lord thy God, and him only shalt thou serve.

Luk 4:18 The Spirit of the Lord [is] upon me, because He hath anointed me to preach the gospel to the poor; He hath sent me to heal the brokenhearted, to preach deliverance to the captives, and recovering of sight to the blind, to set at liberty them that are bruised,

Luk 4:19 To preach the acceptable year of the Lord.

Luk 4:21 And He began to say unto them, This day is this scripture fulfilled in your ears.

Luk 4:24 And He said, Verily I say unto you, No prophet is accepted in his own country.

Luk 4:29 And rose up, and thrust Him out of the city, and led Him unto the brow of the hill whereon their city was built, that they might cast Him down headlong.

Luk 4:30 But He passing through the midst of them went His way,

Luk 4:32 And they were astonished at His doctrine: for His word was with power.

Luk 4:43 And He said unto them, I must preach the kingdom of God to other cities also: for therefore am I sent.

Luk 4:44 And He preached in the synagogues of Galilee.

Mat 16:21 from that time forth began Jesus to shew unto his disciples, how that He must go unto Jerusalem, and suffer many things of the elders and chief priests and scribes, and be killed, and be raised again the third day.

Mat 16:22 Then Peter took him, and began to rebuke him, saying, be it far from thee, Lord: this shall not be unto thee.

Mat 16:23 But He turned, and said unto Peter, Get thee behind Me, Satan: thou art an offence unto Me: for thou savourest not the things that be of God, but those that be of men.

Mat 16:24 Then said Jesus unto his disciples, If any [man] will come after Me, let him deny himself, and take up his cross, and follow Me.

Mat 16:25 For whosoever will save his life shall lose it: and whosoever will lose his life for My sake shall find it.

Mat 16:26 For what is a man profited, if he shall gain the whole world, and lose his own soul? or what shall a man give in exchange for his soul?

Mat 16:27 For the Son of man shall come in the glory of His Father with His angels; and then He shall reward every man according to his works.

Jhn 3:5 Jesus answered, Verily, verily, I say unto thee, Except a man be born of water and [of] the Spirit, he cannot enter into the kingdom of God.

Act 14:22 Confirming the souls of the disciples, [and] exhorting them to continue in the faith, and that we must through much tribulation enter into the kingdom of God.

Hbr 3:11 So I sware in my wrath, They shall not enter into my rest.

Hbr 3:18 And to whom sware he that they should not enter into his rest, but to them that believed not?

Hbr 4:3 For we which have believed do enter into rest, as he said, As I have sworn in my wrath, if they shall enter into my rest: although the works were finished from the foundation of the world.

Hbr 4:5 And in this [place] again, If they shall enter into my rest.

Hbr 4:11 Let us labour therefore to enter into that rest, lest any man fall after the same example of unbelief.

1Cr 5:7 Purge out therefore the old leaven, that ye may be a new lump, as ye are unleavened. For even Christ our passover is sacrificed for us:

1Cr 5:8 Therefore let us keep the feast, not with old leaven, neither with the leaven of malice and wickedness; but with the unleavened [bread] of sincerity and truth.

1Cr 5:9 I wrote unto you in an epistle not to company with fornicators:

1Cr 5:10 Yet not altogether with the fornicators of this world, or with the covetous, or extortioners, or with idolaters; for then must ye needs go out of the world.

The Lamb, Christ, our Passover is sacrificed for us. The Passover Lamb redeemed His brethren, He transcends death. Hold onto the Lamb beyond your strength.

2Cr 12:9 And he said unto me, My grace is sufficient for thee: for my strength is made perfect in weakness.

Most gladly therefore will I rather glory in my infirmities, that the power of Christ may rest upon me. 2Cr 12:10 Therefore I take pleasure in infirmities, in reproaches, in necessities, in persecutions, in distresses for Christ's sake: for when I am weak, then am I strong.
Jhn 1:29 The next day John seeth Jesus coming unto him, and saith, Behold the Lamb of God, which taketh away the sin of the world.

Hbr 10:19 Having therefore, brethren, boldness to enter into the holiest by the blood of Jesus,
Rev 15:8 And the temple was filled with smoke from the glory of God, and from his power; and no man was able to enter into the temple, till the seven plagues of the seven angels were fulfilled.
Rev 21:27 And there shall in no wise enter into it any thing that defileth, neither [whatsoever] worketh abomination, or [maketh] a lie: but they which are written in the Lamb's book of life.
Luk 9:51 and it came to pass, when the time was come that He should be received up, He stedfastly set His face to go to Jerusalem,
Luk 9:53 and they did not receive Him, because His face was as though He would go to Jerusalem.
Luk 18:31 Then He took [unto him] the twelve, and said unto them, Behold, we go up to Jerusalem, and all things that are written by the prophets concerning the Son of man shall be accomplished.
Luk 18:32 for He shall be delivered unto the Gentiles, and shall be mocked, and spitefully entreated, and spitted on:
Luk 18:33 and they shall scourge [Him], and put Him to death: and the third day He shall rise again.
Luk 24:26 Ought not Christ to have suffered these things, and to enter into his glory?

Mar 8:35 For whosoever will save his life shall lose it; but whosoever shall lose his life for my sake and the gospel's, the same shall save it.

Luk 9:24 For whosoever will save his life shall lose it: but whosoever will lose his life for my sake, the same shall save it.

Mar 16:15   And he said unto them, Go ye into all the world, and preach the gospel to every creature.

Mar 16:16   He that believeth and is baptized shall be saved; but he that believeth not shall be damned.

Jhn 3:5 Jesus answered, Verily, verily, I say unto thee, Except a man be born of water and [of] the Spirit, he cannot enter into the kingdom of God.

Jhn 3:6 That which is born of the flesh is flesh; and that which is born of the Spirit is spirit.

Jhn 3:7 Marvel not that I said unto thee, Ye must be born again.

Rev 22:17 And the Spirit and the bride say, Come. And let him that heareth say, Come. And let him that is athirst come. And whosoever will, let him take the water of life freely.

Chapter 7
God is the creator

Jam 1:17 Every good gift and every perfect gift is from above, and cometh down from the Father of lights, with whom is no variableness, neither shadow of turning.

Jam 1:18 Of His own will begat He us with the word of truth, that we should be a kind of firstfruits of His creatures.

Isa 55:11 So shall my word be that goeth forth out of my mouth: it shall not return unto me void, but it shall accomplish that which I please, and it shall prosper [in the thing] whereto I sent it.

Eze 12:25 For I [am] the LORD: I will speak, and the word that I shall speak shall come to pass; it shall be no more prolonged: for in your days, O rebellious house, will I say the word, and will perform it, saith the Lord GOD.

Jhn 1:1 In the beginning was the Word, and the Word was with God, and the Word was God.

Jhn 1:2 The same was in the beginning with God.

Jhn 1:3 All things were made by Him; and without Him was not any thing made that was made.

Jhn 1:4 In Him was life; and the life was the light of men.

Jhn 1:5 And the light shineth in darkness; and the darkness comprehended it not.

Jhn 1:14 And the Word was made flesh, and dwelt among us, (and we beheld his glory, the glory as of the only begotten of the Father,) full of grace and truth.

1Jo 5:7 For there are three that bear record in heaven, the Father, the Word, and the Holy Ghost: and these three are one.

Isa 45:23 I have sworn by myself, the word is gone out of my mouth [in] righteousness, and shall not

return, that unto me every knee shall bow, every tongue shall swear.
Phl 2:10 That at the name of Jesus every knee should bow, of [things] in heaven, and [things] in earth, and [things] under the earth;
Phl 2:11 And [that] every tongue should confess that Jesus Christ [is] Lord, to the glory of God the Father.

Creation is God's spoken Glory

God's Word became flesh and dwelt amongst us. Who made all things; nothing was made without Him.

Hbr 11:3 Through faith we understand that the worlds were framed by the word of God, so that things which are seen were not made of things which do appear.
Gen 1:3 And God said, Let there be light: and there was light.
Gen 1:6 And God said, Let there be a firmament in the midst of the waters, and let it divide the waters from the waters.
Gen 1:9 And God said, Let the waters under the heaven be gathered together unto one place, and let the dry [land] appear: and it was so.
Gen 1:11 And God said, Let the earth bring forth grass, the herb yielding seed, [and] the fruit tree yielding fruit after his kind, whose seed [is] in itself, upon the earth: and it was so.
Gen 1:14 And God said, Let there be lights in the firmament of the heaven to divide the day from the night; and let them be for signs, and for seasons, and for days, and years:
Gen 1:20 And God said, Let the waters bring forth abundantly the moving creature that hath life, and fowl [that] may fly above the earth in the open firmament of heaven.

Gen 1:24 And God said, Let the earth bring forth the living creature after his kind, cattle, and creeping thing, and beast of the earth after his kind: and it was so.

Who, and what we are is witnessed throughout biblical scriptures and still today but in Genesis Adam and Eve are newcreated and pure, "So God created man in His image;", "In the beginning was the Word, and the Word was with God", "For I [am] the LORD: I will speak, and the word that I shall speak shall come to pass;", "For God, who commanded the light to shine out of darkness" and "He made him in the likeness of God" and "He created them male and female." Scripture displays the power of God's Spirit, His perfect will that accomplishes creation by His Word of truth.

The Purpose for Human Life is Pending

1Cr 13:12 For now we see through a glass, darkly; but then face to face: now I know in part; but then shall I know even as also I am known.

Gen 1:26 And God said, Let us make man in our image, after our likeness: and let them have dominion over the fish of the sea, and over the fowl of the air, and over the cattle, and over all the earth, and over every creeping thing that creepeth upon the earth.
Gen 1:27 So God created man in his [own] image, in the image of God created he him; male and female created he them.
Gen 1:31 And God saw every thing that he had made, and, behold, [it was] very good. And the evening and the morning were the sixth day.
Gen 2:7 And the LORD God formed man [of] the dust of the ground, and breathed into his nostrils the breath of life; and man became a living soul.

Gen 5:1 This [is] the book of the generations of Adam. In the day that God created man, in the likeness of God made he him;
Gen 5:2 Male and female created he them; and blessed them, and called their name Adam, in the day when they were created.

We are the descendants of all our parents, the genetic, cultural and spiritual. We are not familiar with the will of God and so then are unlikely to recognize the components of His image even though some must remain and are seen each time we look on another person. We do not look for the image of God throughout our daily discourse. We do not perceive, are not aware of the condition of human being. There are few clues to enable a pre historical evaluation of human consciousness to steer the consideration of the origin of our existence. The sophistication of the apostles' reasoning is witness to profound thought that survived only due to the severe nature of the message. God's truth and delivered promise, the redemption message was so unique it survived contention and the meager communication practices of that era. The paradoxical question, what came first the chicken or the egg, taunts our understanding and theories of ancient human history and the crux of our purpose, who we are. Creation or evolution is the contemporary turn of that concept. Inanimate elements or molecules do not coalesce into living organisms. Was slime cooked, pushed and pulled enough for our likeness? Stretching out the transition from slime to humanity over huge clusters of time is nothing more than the application of a curtain to hide the impossible. How many in human history were formed of the dust and animated by the breath of life? Human being was not an accident. There is a purpose to human life that is pending. Multitudes of lives have been necessary to obtain a sufficient number for His purpose.

The Image and Likeness of God

What is the image and likeness of God? The answer to this question is contrary to our lives and so is hardly comprehendible to those of the flesh. Suspend evaluation that has no comparator in this matter. God is not many as some propose due to the word, "us" in verse 26 of the first Genesis chapter and verses 3:22, and 11:7. Multiple verses proclaim that there is one God. Deut 6:4 – 9, Isa 44:6 – 8, 45:5, 6, 45: 21 – 23, 46:8, 9, Mark 12:29, 32, Acts 20:28, 1Cor 4:4 – 6, Eph 4:5, 6, 1Tim 2:5, James 2:19, Rev 4:2, 3. The "us" of Genesis then provides insight into the mystery of God.

1Jo 5:7 For there are three that bear record in heaven, the Father, the Word, and the Holy Ghost: and these three are one. 2Cor 5:18-21, John 1:3, Zec 4:6, Mark 3:28-30

Rev 5:12 Saying with a loud voice, Worthy is the Lamb that was slain to receive power, and riches, and wisdom, and strength, and honour, and glory, and blessing.

Rev 5:13 And every creature which is in heaven, and on the earth, and under the earth, and such as are in the sea, and all that are in them, heard I saying, Blessing, and honour, and glory, and power, [be] unto him that sitteth upon the throne, and unto the Lamb for ever and ever.

Rev 6:1 And I saw when the Lamb opened one of the seals, and I heard, as it were the noise of thunder, one of the four beasts saying, Come and see.

Rev 21:22 And I saw no temple therein: for the Lord God Almighty and the Lamb are the temple of it.

Rev 21:23 And the city had no need of the sun, neither of the moon, to shine in it: for the glory of God did lighten it, and the Lamb [is] the light thereof.

Rev 21:27 And there shall in no wise enter into it any thing that defileth, neither [whatsoever] worketh abomination, or [maketh] a lie: but they which are written in the Lamb's book of life.
Rev 22:1 And he shewed me a pure river of water of life, clear as crystal, proceeding out of the throne of God and of the Lamb.
Rev 22:3 And there shall be no more curse: but the throne of God and of the Lamb shall be in it; and his servants shall serve him:

Mystery of Godliness for Beings that Die

There are 3 that bear record in heaven, "the Father, the Word and the Holy Ghost: and these three are one." There is the Lamb, "a pure river of water of life, clear as crystal, proceeding out of the throne of God and of the Lamb". The Lamb is the glory of God, "for the glory of God did lighten it, and the Lamb [is] the light thereof." "Lamb" is used 29 times in the last book of the bible, "the Lamb" occurs 26 times. There are various beings, angels, beasts and saints in the presence of the Creator. The Creator is spirit, communes in spirit with beings of spirit who inhabit any form or body convenient for the purposes of the Creator, God. Spirit, the deathless, recognize events, decisions and spirit beings in an alien and superhuman manner to our limited perception. Time nor aging are involved, neither are their forms constrained. The expression of their choices, their being is recognized in a befitting form. Jesus is the Lamb of God.

The world hastens to deny the deity of Jesus. Many can be heard bemoaning those who have made Jesus more than a man, elevating Him to God. Scripture declares Jesus is God and Son of man. Scripture also identifies the spirit of antichrist. That spirit is so very bold it deflects; defeats the testimony of many who would believe God.

1Jo 4:3 And every spirit that confesseth not that Jesus Christ is come in the flesh is not of God: and this is that [spirit] of antichrist, whereof ye have heard that it should come; and even now already is it in the world.
Col 2:2 That their hearts might be comforted, being knit together in love, and unto all riches of the full assurance of understanding, to the acknowledgement of the mystery of God, and of the Father, and of Christ;
Act 4:26 The kings of the earth stood up, and the rulers were gathered together against the Lord, and against his Christ.
Rev 11:15 And the seventh angel sounded; and there were great voices in heaven, saying, The kingdoms of this world are become [the kingdoms] of our Lord, and of his Christ; and he shall reign for ever and ever.
Rev 12:10 And I heard a loud voice saying in heaven, Now is come salvation, and strength, and the kingdom of our God, and the power of his Christ: for the accuser of our brethren is cast down, which accused them before our God day and night.

1Ti 3:16 And without controversy great is the mystery of godliness: God was manifest in the flesh, justified in the Spirit, seen of angels, preached unto the Gentiles, believed on in the world, received up into glory.
Eph 3:9 And to make all [men] see what [is] the fellowship of the mystery, which from the beginning of the world hath been hid in God, who created all things by Jesus Christ:
2Cr 4:3 But if our gospel be hid, it is hid to them that are lost:
2Cr 4:4 In whom the god of this world hath blinded the minds of them which believe not, lest the light of the glorious gospel of Christ, who is the image of God, should shine unto them.

2Cr 4:5 For we preach not ourselves, but Christ Jesus the Lord; and ourselves your servants for Jesus' sake.

1Cr 2:4 And my speech and my preaching [was] not with enticing words of man's wisdom, but in demonstration of the Spirit and of power:
1Cr 2:5 That your faith should not stand in the wisdom of men, but in the power of God.
1Cr 2:6 Howbeit we speak wisdom among them that are perfect: yet not the wisdom of this world, nor of the princes of this world, that come to nought:
1Cr 2:7 But we speak the wisdom of God in a mystery, [even] the hidden [wisdom], which God ordained before the world unto our glory:
1Cr 2:8 Which none of the princes of this world knew: for had they known [it], they would not have crucified the Lord of glory.
1Cr 2:9 But as it is written, Eye hath not seen, nor ear heard, neither have entered into the heart of man, the things which God hath prepared for them that love him.
1Cr 2:10 But God hath revealed [them] unto us by his Spirit: for the Spirit searcheth all things, yea, the deep things of God.
1Cr 2:11 For what man knoweth the things of a man, save the spirit of man which is in him? even so the things of God knoweth no man, but the Spirit of God.
1Cr 2:12 Now we have received, not the spirit of the world, but the spirit which is of God; that we might know the things that are freely given to us of God.
1Cr 2:13 Which things also we speak, not in the words which man's wisdom teacheth, but which the Holy Ghost teacheth; comparing spiritual things with spiritual.
1Cr 2:14 But the natural man receiveth not the things of the Spirit of God: for they are foolishness unto him:

neither can he know [them], because they are spiritually discerned.
Rev 10:7 But in the days of the voice of the seventh angel, when he shall begin to sound, the mystery of God should be finished, as he hath declared to his servants the prophets.

The testimony of Jesus is the spirit of prophecy

Rev 19:10 And I fell at his feet to worship him. And he said unto me, See [thou do it] not: I am thy fellowservant, and of thy brethren that have the testimony of Jesus: worship God: for the testimony of Jesus is the spirit of prophecy.
Rev 1:2 Who bare record of the word of God, and of the testimony of Jesus Christ, and of all things that he saw.
Rev 1:7 Behold, he cometh with clouds; and every eye shall see him, and they [also] which pierced him: and all kindreds of the earth shall wail because of him. Even so, Amen.
Rev 1:8 I am Alpha and Omega, the beginning and the ending, saith the Lord, which is, and which was, and which is to come, the Almighty.
Rev 1:9 I John, who also am your brother, and companion in tribulation, and in the kingdom and patience of Jesus Christ, was in the isle that is called Patmos, for the word of God, and for the testimony of Jesus Christ.

Rev 1:13 And in the midst of the seven candlesticks [one] like unto the Son of man, clothed with a garment down to the foot, and girt about the paps with a golden girdle.
Rev 1:14 His head and [his] hairs [were] white like wool, as white as snow; and his eyes [were] as a flame of fire;

Rev 1:15 And his feet like unto fine brass, as if they burned in a furnace; and his voice as the sound of many waters.

Rev 1:16 And he had in his right hand seven stars: and out of his mouth went a sharp twoedged sword: and his countenance [was] as the sun shineth in his strength.

Rev 1:17 And when I saw him, I fell at his feet as dead. And he laid his right hand upon me, saying unto me, Fear not; I am the first and the last:

Rev 1:18 I [am] he that liveth, and was dead; and, behold, I am alive for evermore, Amen; and have the keys of hell and of death.

Rev 1:19 Write the things which thou hast seen, and the things which are, and the things which shall be hereafter;

Rev 12:1 And there appeared a great wonder in heaven; a woman clothed with the sun, and the moon under her feet, and upon her head a crown of twelve stars:

Rev 12:2 And she being with child cried, travailing in birth, and pained to be delivered.

Rev 12:3 And there appeared another wonder in heaven; and behold a great red dragon, having seven heads and ten horns, and seven crowns upon his heads.

Rev 12:4 And his tail drew the third part of the stars of heaven, and did cast them to the earth: and the dragon stood before the woman which was ready to be delivered, for to devour her child as soon as it was born.

Rev 12:5 And she brought forth a man child, who was to rule all nations with a rod of iron: and her child was caught up unto God, and [to] his throne.

Rev 12:17 And the dragon was wroth with the woman, and went to make war with the remnant of her seed, which keep the commandments of God, and have the testimony of Jesus Christ.

Rev 19:11 And I saw heaven opened, and behold a white horse; and he that sat upon him [was] called Faithful and True, and in righteousness he doth judge and make war.

Rev 19:12 His eyes [were] as a flame of fire, and on his head [were] many crowns; and he had a name written, that no man knew, but he himself.

Rev 19:13 And he [was] clothed with a vesture dipped in blood: and his name is called The Word of God.

Act 4:24 And when they heard that, they lifted up their voice to God with one accord, and said, Lord, thou [art] God, which hast made heaven, and earth, and the sea, and all that in them is:

Act 4:25 Who by the mouth of thy servant David hast said, Why did the heathen rage, and the people imagine vain things?

Act 4:26 The kings of the earth stood up, and the rulers were gathered together against the Lord, and against his Christ.

Act 4:27 For of a truth against thy holy child Jesus, whom thou hast anointed, both Herod, and Pontius Pilate, with the Gentiles, and the people of Israel, were gathered together,

Act 4:28 For to do whatsoever thy hand and thy counsel determined before to be done.

Act 4:29 And now, Lord, behold their threatenings: and grant unto thy servants, that with all boldness they may speak thy word,

Act 4:30 By stretching forth thine hand to heal; and that signs and wonders may be done by the name of thy holy child Jesus.

Act 4:31 And when they had prayed, the place was shaken where they were assembled together; and they were all filled with the Holy Ghost, and they spake the word of God with boldness.

Jhn 15:4 Abide in me, and I in you. As the branch cannot bear fruit of itself, except it abide in the vine; no more can ye, except ye abide in me.

Jhn 15:5 I am the vine, ye [are] the branches: He that abideth in me, and I in him, the same bringeth forth much fruit: for without me ye can do nothing.

Jhn 15:6 If a man abide not in me, he is cast forth as a branch, and is withered; and men gather them, and cast [them] into the fire, and they are burned.

Jhn 15:7 If ye abide in me, and my words abide in you, ye shall ask what ye will, and it shall be done unto you.

Jhn 15:8 Herein is my Father glorified, that ye bear much fruit; so shall ye be my disciples.

Jhn 15:9 As the Father hath loved me, so have I loved you: continue ye in my love.

Jhn 15:10 If ye keep my commandments, ye shall abide in my love; even as I have kept my Father's commandments, and abide in his love.

Jhn 15:11 These things have I spoken unto you, that my joy might remain in you, and [that] your joy might be full.

Jhn 15:12 This is my commandment, That ye love one another, as I have loved you.

Jhn 15:13 Greater love hath no man than this, that a man lay down his life for his friends.

Jhn 15:14 Ye are my friends, if ye do whatsoever I command you.

Jhn 15:15 Henceforth I call you not servants; for the servant knoweth not what his lord doeth: but I have called you friends; for all things that I have heard of my Father I have made known unto you.

Jhn 15:16 Ye have not chosen me, but I have chosen you, and ordained you, that ye should go and bring forth fruit, and [that] your fruit should remain: that whatsoever ye shall ask of the Father in my name, he may give it you.

Jhn 15:17 These things I command you, that ye love one another.

Jhn 15:18 If the world hate you, ye know that it hated me before [it hated] you.

Jhn 15:19 If ye were of the world, the world would love his own: but because ye are not of the world, but I have chosen you out of the world, therefore the world hateth you.

Jhn 15:20 Remember the word that I said unto you, The servant is not greater than his lord. If they have persecuted me, they will also persecute you; if they have kept my saying, they will keep yours also.

Jhn 15:21 But all these things will they do unto you for my name's sake, because they know not him that sent me.

Jhn 15:22 If I had not come and spoken unto them, they had not had sin: but now they have no cloke for their sin.

Jhn 15:23 He that hateth me hateth my Father also.

Jhn 15:24 If I had not done among them the works which none other man did, they had not had sin: but now have they both seen and hated both me and my Father.

Jhn 15:25 But [this cometh to pass], that the word might be fulfilled that is written in their law, They hated me without a cause.

Jhn 15:26 But when the Comforter is come, whom I will send unto you from the Father, [even] the Spirit of truth, which proceedeth from the Father, he shall testify of me:

Dan 7:13 I saw in the night visions, and, behold, [one] like the Son of man came with the clouds of heaven, and came to the Ancient of days, and they brought him near before him.

Dan 7:14 And there was given him dominion, and glory, and a kingdom, that all people, nations, and languages, should serve him: his dominion [is] an everlasting dominion, which shall not pass away, and his kingdom [that] which shall not be destroyed.

Dan 7:21 I beheld, and the same horn made war with the saints, and prevailed against them;
Dan 7:22 Until the Ancient of days came, and judgment was given to the saints of the most High; and the time came that the saints possessed the kingdom.
Dan 7:25 And he shall speak [great] words against the most High, and shall wear out the saints of the most High, and think to change times and laws: and they shall be given into his hand until a time and times and the dividing of time.
Dan 7:26 But the judgment shall sit, and they shall take away his dominion, to consume and to destroy [it] unto the end.
Dan 7:27 And the kingdom and dominion, and the greatness of the kingdom under the whole heaven, shall be given to the people of the saints of the most High, whose kingdom [is] an everlasting kingdom, and all dominions shall serve and obey him.
Luk 12:4 And I say unto you my friends, Be not afraid of them that kill the body, and after that have no more that they can do.
Luk 12:5 But I will forewarn you whom ye shall fear: Fear Him, which after He hath killed hath power to cast into hell; yea, I say unto you, Fear Him.
Rev 4:8 And the four beasts had each of them six wings about [him]; and [they were] full of eyes within: and they rest not day and night, saying, Holy, holy, holy, Lord God Almighty, which was, and is, and is to come.

Devour, a sharp two edged sword, war, persecution, the heathen rage, tribulation, the world hated me before you, if the world

persecuted me, they will also persecute you, antichrist

The only God is known to creation in 3 ways. Satan contends that there is more than one God. The mystery of God, the outcome of creation is the testimony of Jesus. The bible, the book of human creation states that the testimony of Jesus is the spirit of prophecy. Prophecy, "which was, and is, and is to come" is the testimony of Jesus who is the first and the last and who holds the keys of hell and death. Jesus is the first who was ordained before the foundation of the world and the last. The last excludes any other; there is none else, there is no other way. No wonder the dragon sought to devour the child and makes war with those that keep the commandments of God and have the testimony of Jesus Christ. The heathen rage, the kings of the earth and the rulers gather against the Lord and His Christ. Jesus is the Alpha and Omega which is, and which was, and which is to come, the Almighty. Jesus is the Lamb of God.

Jam 1:17 Every good gift and every perfect gift is from above, and cometh down from the Father of lights, with whom is no variableness, neither shadow of turning.
Mar 12:32 And the scribe said unto him, Well, Master, thou hast said the truth: for there is one God; and there is none other but he:
1Cr 8:3 But if any man love God, the same is known of him.
1Cr 8:4 As concerning therefore the eating of those things that are offered in sacrifice unto idols, we know that an idol [is] nothing in the world, and that [there is] none other God but one.
1Cr 8:5 For though there be that are called gods, whether in heaven or in earth, (as there be gods many, and lords many,)

1Cr 8:6 But to us [there is but] one God, the Father, of whom [are] all things, and we in him; and one Lord Jesus Christ, by whom [are] all things, and we by him.
2Cr 1:18 But [as] God [is] true, our word toward you was not yea and nay.
2Cr 1:19 For the Son of God, Jesus Christ, who was preached among you by us, [even] by me and Silvanus and Timotheus, was not yea and nay, but in him was yea.
2Cr 1:20 For all the promises of God in him [are] yea, and in him Amen, unto the glory of God by us.
2Cr 1:21 Now he which stablisheth us with you in Christ, and hath anointed us, [is] God;
2Cr 1:22 Who hath also sealed us, and given the earnest of the Spirit in our hearts.
Act 4:12 Neither is there salvation in any other: for there is none other name under heaven given among men, whereby we must be saved.

How many in human history were conceived by the Holy Spirit?

There can be but one, "only begotten".

Jhn 1:14 And the Word was made flesh, and dwelt among us, (and we beheld His glory, the glory as of the only begotten of the Father,) full of grace and truth.
Luk 1:34 Then said Mary unto the angel, How shall this be, seeing I know not a man?
Luk 1:35 And the angel answered and said unto her, The Holy Ghost shall come upon thee, and the power of the Highest shall overshadow thee: therefore also that holy thing which shall be born of thee shall be called the Son of God.
Also Matthew 1:18

Mat 22:30 For in the resurrection they neither marry, nor are given in marriage, but are as the angels of God in heaven.
Also Mark 12:25

Jhn 1:12 But as many as received him, to them gave he power to become the sons of God, [even] to them that believe on his name:
Jhn 1:13 Which were born, not of blood, nor of the will of the flesh, nor of the will of man, but of God.

We know the extremity that is to be like Jesus. Who we are now, what Adam and Eve chose, almost cannot accept the truth, or reconcile the condition of our separation from God. The human experience has produced lost beings. Erased from any relational memory of what those in the image of God were we barely discern God's pleading to accept the role and existence human was and will be. We watch the drama of our own life yet do not turn the corner to arrive at the next level. The challenge of spiritual existence is unattainable for inherent ignorance of this presence. True human being must be revealed to those who seek reunion with their creator. Made in the image of God is how this occurs. Flesh cannot acquire that which cannot be touched or perceived.

Psa 103:14 For he knoweth our frame; he remembereth that we [are] dust.
Psa 103:15 [As for] man, his days [are] as grass: as a flower of the field, so he flourisheth.
Psa 103:16 For the wind passeth over it, and it is gone; and the place thereof shall know it no more.
Psa 103:17 But the mercy of the LORD [is] from everlasting to everlasting upon them that fear him, and his righteousness unto children's children;
Isa 40:6 The voice said, Cry. And he said, What shall I cry? All flesh [is] grass, and all the goodliness thereof [is] as the flower of the field:

Isa 40:7 The grass withereth, the flower fadeth: because the spirit of the LORD bloweth upon it: surely the people [is] grass.
Isa 40:8 The grass withereth, the flower fadeth: but the word of our God shall stand for ever.
Jhn 3:12 If I have told you earthly things, and ye believe not, how shall ye believe, if I tell you [of] heavenly things?
Jhn 3:13 And no man hath ascended up to heaven, but he that came down from heaven, [even] the Son of man which is in heaven.
Eph 2:12 That at that time ye were without Christ, being aliens from the commonwealth of Israel, and strangers from the covenants of promise, having no hope, and without God in the world:

Spiritual Preeminence

Our realm, earth, water and air condition our thoughts and perception. Our thoughts are chronologically ordered, conforming to our experience as we progress from our first moments of awareness onto our expiration. Adam and Eve became aware of who they were when they ingested the forbidden fruit, thereby committing their heirs to a personal focus relating to the physical world in which humanity dwells. Strange culture, customs and traditions of isolated groups faintly suggest how distant physical beings are from spiritual conception. Humanity is stuck in tunnel vision.

1Cr 13:12 For now we see through a glass, darkly; but then face to face: now I know in part; but then shall I know even as also I am known.
Jhn 14:17 [Even] the Spirit of truth; whom the world cannot receive, because it seeth him not, neither knoweth him: but ye know him; for he dwelleth with you, and shall be in you.

Rom 8:26 Likewise the Spirit also helpeth our infirmities: for we know not what we should pray for as we ought: but the Spirit itself maketh intercession for us with groanings which cannot be uttered.

Humans taste desire and learn to ride lust when they reject God. The effects of the forbidden taking are degenerative and destructive. Genesis displays human interaction apart from God with but few exceptional souls calling on and heeding their Creator. The Genesis book could have been a joyous celebration rather than a tragic account of humanity. The human display revealed throughout Genesis is physical and naturally so as people of this world do confirm.

1Cr 2:11 For what man knoweth the things of a man, save the spirit of man which is in him? even so the things of God knoweth no man, but the Spirit of God.

We do know the way of this world as confirmed historically and in current events. Genesis is a physical display to provide contrast sufficient to help humans living in the physical to comprehend the way of the spirit; to begin to see the will of God. Scripture insists that we must be led by the spirit. Adam and Eve were created in the image of God. God is a spirit. Our Creator yearns for us to partake fully of His blessing and life. The lost component of our being is that which is disdained by the world, yet His spirit can now be renewed. Jesus is the image of what humans were and are to be.

2Cr 4:4 In whom the god of this world hath blinded the minds of them which believe not, lest the light of the glorious gospel of Christ, who is the image of God, should shine unto them.

God's disappointment and sorrow in the garden was the severing of His Spirit, the essence of God from Adam and Eve. God offers to "renew" the gift of the Holy Ghost. God is not limited by the impossible; He is the creator/recreator. Now is the time provided for His children to choose Him. Satan and all who practice denial of God believe a lie and the truth is not in them. Their choices that determine who they are separate them from God.

2Cr 6:2 (For he saith, I have heard thee in a time accepted, and in the day of salvation have I succoured thee: behold, now [is] the accepted time; behold, now [is] the day of salvation.)
Tts 3:4 But after that the kindness and love of God our Saviour toward man appeared,
Tts 3:5 Not by works of righteousness which we have done, but according to his mercy he saved us, by the washing of regeneration, and renewing of the Holy Ghost;
Tts 3:6 Which he shed on us abundantly through Jesus Christ our Saviour;
Tts 3:7 That being justified by his grace, we should be made heirs according to the hope of eternal life.
2Cr 3:18 But we all, with open face beholding as in a glass the glory of the Lord, are changed into the same image from glory to glory, [even] as by the Spirit of the Lord.
2Cr 4:6 For God, who commanded the light to shine out of darkness, hath shined in our hearts, to [give] the light of the knowledge of the glory of God in the face of Jesus Christ.
2Cr 4:7 But we have this treasure in earthen vessels, that the excellency of the power may be of God, and not of us.
Phl 3:21 Who shall change our vile body, that it may be fashioned like unto his glorious body, according to the working whereby he is able even to subdue all things unto himself.
Act 26:23 That Christ should suffer, [and] that he should be the first that should rise from the dead, and should shew light unto the people, and to the Gentiles.

Rev 1:5 And from Jesus Christ, [who is] the faithful witness, [and] the first begotten of the dead, and the prince of the kings of the earth. Unto him that loved us, and washed us from our sins in his own blood,

1Th 4:16 For the Lord himself shall descend from heaven with a shout, with the voice of the archangel, and with the trump of God: and the dead in Christ shall rise first:

Rom 8:2 For the law of the Spirit of life in Christ Jesus hath made me free from the law of sin and death.

Rom 8:3 For what the law could not do, in that it was weak through the flesh, God sending his own Son in the likeness of sinful flesh, and for sin, condemned sin in the flesh:

Rom 8:4   That the righteousness of the law might be fulfilled in us, who walk not after the flesh, but after the Spirit.

Rom 8:5 For they that are after the flesh do mind the things of the flesh; but they that are after the Spirit the things of the Spirit.

Rom 8:6 For to be carnally minded [is] death; but to be spiritually minded [is] life and peace.

Rom 8:7 Because the carnal mind [is] enmity against God: for it is not subject to the law of God, neither indeed can be.

Rom 8:8 So then they that are in the flesh cannot please God.

Rom 8:9 But ye are not in the flesh, but in the Spirit, if so be that the Spirit of God dwell in you. Now if any man have not the Spirit of Christ, he is none of His.

Jhn 3:5 Jesus answered, Verily, verily, I say unto thee, Except a man be born of water and [of] the Spirit, he cannot enter into the kingdom of God.

Jhn 3:6 That which is born of the flesh is flesh; and that which is born of the Spirit is spirit.

Jhn 3:7 Marvel not that I said unto thee, Ye must be born again.

Jhn 14:17 [Even] the Spirit of truth; whom the world cannot receive, because it seeth Him not, neither knoweth Him: but ye know Him; for He dwelleth with you, and shall be in you.
Jhn 14:18 I will not leave you comfortless: I will come to you.
Rom 8:11 But if the Spirit of Him that raised up Jesus from the dead dwell in you,
He that raised up Christ from the dead shall also quicken your mortal bodies by His Spirit that dwelleth in you.
Rom 8:12 Therefore, brethren, we are debtors, not to the flesh, to live after the flesh.
Rom 8:13 For if ye live after the flesh, ye shall die: but if ye through the Spirit do mortify the deeds of the body, ye shall live.
Rom 8:14 For as many as are led by the Spirit of God, they are the sons of God.
Rom 8:15 For ye have not received the spirit of bondage again to fear; but ye have received the Spirit of adoption, whereby we cry, Abba, Father.
Rom 8:16 The Spirit itself beareth witness with our spirit, that we are the children of God:
1Cr 3:16 Know ye not that ye are the temple of God, and [that] the Spirit of God dwelleth in you?
2Ti 1:14 That good thing which was committed unto thee keep by the Holy Ghost which dwelleth in us.

Utter Treasure Must be Gifted

We can live this treasure in our earthen vessels. Life cannot be purchased. It may be recovered from disease or continued through repair but death is sure. The Spirit of God does not simply occur or cannot be purchased; it is the presence of our Creator. God indwells His children who are His image. Treasure, precious, totally beyond our capabilities, incorruptible it is the promise for those who choose God.

Luk 24:49 And, behold, I send the promise of my Father upon you: but tarry ye in the city of Jerusalem, until ye be endued with power from on high.

Act 1:4 And, being assembled together with [them], commanded them that they should not depart from Jerusalem, but wait for the promise of the Father, which, [saith he], ye have heard of me.

Act 2:33 Therefore being by the right hand of God exalted, and having received of the Father the promise of the Holy Ghost, he hath shed forth this, which ye now see and hear.

Act 2:39 For the promise is unto you, and to your children, and to all that are afar off, [even] as many as the Lord our God shall call.

Act 7:17 But when the time of the promise drew nigh, which God had sworn to Abraham, the people grew and multiplied in Egypt,

Act 13:32 And we declare unto you glad tidings, how that the promise which was made unto the fathers,

Act 26:6 And now I stand and am judged for the hope of the promise made of God unto our fathers:

Rom 4:13 For the promise, that he should be the heir of the world, [was] not to Abraham, or to his seed, through the law, but through the righteousness of faith.

Rom 4:14 For if they which are of the law [be] heirs, faith is made void, and the promise made of none effect:

Rom 4:16 Therefore [it is] of faith, that [it might be] by grace; to the end the promise might be sure to all the seed; not to that only which is of the law, but to that also which is of the faith of Abraham; who is the father of us all,

Rom 4:20 He staggered not at the promise of God through unbelief; but was strong in faith, giving glory to God;

Rom 9:8 That is, They which are the children of the flesh, these [are] not the children of God: but the children of the promise are counted for the seed.

Gal 3:14 That the blessing of Abraham might come on the Gentiles through Jesus Christ; that we might receive the promise of the Spirit through faith.

Gal 3:17 And this I say, [that] the covenant, that was confirmed before of God in Christ, the law, which was four hundred and thirty years after, cannot disannul, that it should make the promise of none effect.

Gal 3:19 Wherefore then [serveth] the law? It was added because of transgressions, till the seed should come to whom the promise was made; [and it was] ordained by angels in the hand of a mediator.

Gal 3:22 But the scripture hath concluded all under sin, that the promise by faith of Jesus Christ might be given to them that believe.

Gal 3:29 And if ye [be] Christ's, then are ye Abraham's seed, and heirs according to the promise.

2Ti 1:1 Paul, an apostle of Jesus Christ by the will of God, according to the promise of life which is in Christ Jesus,

Hbr 6:15 And so, after he had patiently endured, he obtained the promise.

Hbr 9:15 And for this cause he is the mediator of the new testament, that by means of death, for the redemption of the transgressions [that were] under the first testament, they which are called might receive the promise of eternal inheritance.

Hbr 10:36 For ye have need of patience, that, after ye have done the will of God, ye might receive the promise.

Hbr 11:39 And these all, having obtained a good report through faith, received not the promise:

2Pe 3:4 And saying, Where is the promise of his coming? for since the fathers fell asleep, all things continue as [they were] from the beginning of the creation.

1Jo 2:25 And this is the promise that he hath promised us, [even] eternal life.

Rev 3:20   Behold, I stand at the door, and knock: if any man hear my voice, and open the door, I will come in to him, and will sup with him, and he with me.

Dan 10:5 Then I lifted up mine eyes, and looked, and behold a certain man clothed in linen, whose loins [were] girded with fine gold of Uphaz:

Dan 10:6 His body also [was] like the beryl, and his face as the appearance of lightning, and his eyes as lamps of fire, and his arms and his feet like in colour to polished brass, and the voice of his words like the voice of a multitude.

Dan 10:7 And I Daniel alone saw the vision: for the men that were with me saw not the vision; but a great quaking fell upon them, so that they fled to hide themselves.

Dan 10:8 Therefore I was left alone, and saw this great vision, and there remained no strength in me: for my comeliness was turned in me into corruption, and I retained no strength.

Dan 10:9 Yet heard I the voice of his words: and when I heard the voice of his words, then was I in a deep sleep on my face, and my face toward the ground.

Dan 10:10 And, behold, an hand touched me, which set me upon my knees and [upon] the palms of my hands.

Dan 10:11 And he said unto me, O Daniel, a man greatly beloved, understand the words that I speak unto thee, and stand upright: for unto thee am I now sent. And when he had spoken this word unto me, I stood trembling.

Exd 3:4 And when the LORD saw that he turned aside to see, God called unto him out of the midst of the bush, and said, Moses, Moses. And he said, Here [am] I.

Exd 3:5 And He said, Draw not nigh hither: put off thy shoes from off thy feet, for the place whereon thou standest [is] holy ground.

Exd 3:6 Moreover He said, I [am] the God of thy father, the God of Abraham, the God of Isaac, and the God of Jacob. And Moses hid his face; for he was afraid to look upon God.

2Ch 7:1 Now when Solomon had made an end of praying, the fire came down from heaven, and consumed the burnt offering and the sacrifices; and the glory of the LORD filled the house.

2Ch 7:2 And the priests could not enter into the house of the LORD, because the glory of the LORD had filled the LORD'S house.

Isa 45:5 I [am] the LORD, and [there is] none else, [there is] no God beside me: I girded thee, though thou hast not known Me:

Rom 3:10 As it is written, There is none righteous, no, not one:

Rom 3:11 There is none that understandeth, there is none that seeketh after God.

Rom 3:12 They are all gone out of the way, they are together become unprofitable; there is none that doeth good, no, not one.

Act 8:18 And when Simon saw that through laying on of the apostles' hands the Holy Ghost was given, he offered them money,

Act 8:19 Saying, Give me also this power, that on whomsoever I lay hands, he may receive the Holy Ghost.

Act 8:20 But Peter said unto him, Thy money perish with thee, because thou hast thought that the gift of God may be purchased with money.

Act 8:21 Thou hast neither part nor lot in this matter: for thy heart is not right in the sight of God.
Act 8:22 Repent therefore of this thy wickedness, and pray God, if perhaps the thought of thine heart may be forgiven thee.
Act 8:23 For I perceive that thou art in the gall of bitterness, and [in] the bond of iniquity.

Chapter 8
God Alone

Gen 4:26 And to Seth, to him also there was born a son; and he called his name Enos: then began men to call upon the name of the LORD.
Rom 10:13 For whosoever shall call upon the name of the Lord shall be saved.

Gen 8:21 and the LORD smelled a sweet savour; and the LORD said in his heart, I will not again curse the ground any more for man's sake; for the imagination of man's heart [is] evil from his youth; neither will I again smite any more every thing living, as I have done.
Gen 9:1 And God blessed Noah and his sons, and said unto them, Be fruitful, and multiply, and replenish the earth.
Gen 9:2 And the fear of you and the dread of you shall be upon every beast of the earth, and upon every fowl of the air, upon all that moveth [upon] the earth, and upon all the fishes of the sea; into your hand are they delivered.
Gen 9:3 Every moving thing that liveth shall be meat for you; even as the green herb have I given you all things.
Gen 9:4 But flesh with the life thereof, [which is] the blood thereof, shall ye not eat.
Gen 9:5 And surely your blood of your lives will I require; at the hand of every beast will I require it, and at the hand of man; at the hand of every man's brother will I require the life of man.
Gen 9:6 Whoso sheddeth man's blood, by man shall his blood be shed: for in the image of God made he man.
Gen 9:7 And you, be ye fruitful, and multiply; bring forth abundantly in the earth, and multiply therein.

Gen 10:32 These [are] the families of the sons of Noah, after their generations, in their nations: and by these were the nations divided in the earth after the flood.

All humanity was destroyed but for 8 people. The fresh start on the cleansed earth proceeded to reveal the inability of humans to overcome sin. Desire is an insatiable siren. There will never be enough for those who desire. Survivors of the flood must be re-forbidden to shed blood. The excess that was destroyed was not example enough. The magnitude of the flood event was not example enough. The whole earth is not enough for people of the flesh. This is the last human experiment to prove the fruit, the worth of humanism. The worth or futility of human being without the Spirit of God was reset and proves beyond doubt. The human display confirms in this new\last start of the failure cycle all are hopeless victims of sin apart from God. The many wages of sin are death. At the end of time the judgment is revelation of self or the image of God, those who choose Jesus and those without His Spirit. The lineage of Seth exhibits the behavior where faith, the seed of God's glory, blooms as men call upon the name of the Lord. None would call on the name of the Lord unless they believe. There is no hope for creation, for deliverance or redemption without God.

Hbr 11:6 But without faith [it is] impossible to please [Him]: for he that cometh to God must believe that He is, and [that] He is a rewarder of them that diligently seek Him.
2Pe 2:5 And spared not the old world, but saved Noah the eighth [person], a preacher of righteousness, bringing in the flood upon the world of the ungodly;
Rom 10:13 For whosoever shall call upon the name of the Lord shall be saved.
Rom 10:14 How then shall they call on Him in whom they have not believed? and how shall they believe in

Him of whom they have not heard? and how shall they hear without a preacher?

Rom 10:15 And how shall they preach, except they be sent? as it is written, How beautiful are the feet of them that preach the gospel of peace, and bring glad tidings of good things!

Rom 10:16 But they have not all obeyed the gospel. For Esaias saith, Lord, who hath believed our report?

Rom 10:17 So then faith [cometh] by hearing, and hearing by the word of God.

Rom 10:18 But I say, Have they not heard? Yes verily, their sound went into all the earth, and their words unto the ends of the world.

Rom 10:19 But I say, Did not Israel know? First Moses saith, I will provoke you to jealousy by [them that are] no people, [and] by a foolish nation I will anger you.

Rom 10:20 But Esaias is very bold, and saith, I was found of them that sought me not; I was made manifest unto them that asked not after me.

Rom 10:21 But to Israel he saith, All day long I have stretched forth my hands unto a disobedient and gainsaying people.

Eph 2:12 That at that time ye were without Christ, being aliens from the commonwealth of Israel, and strangers from the covenants of promise, having no hope, and without God in the world:

Neither will they be persuaded, though one rose from the dead

Perspective is a comfortable position and a useful tool for merchants and politicians. It is a deadly counterfeit of reality much like a person backing up at a cliff edge. The condition, the word rich is perspective's twin. Many would agree that the rich should be taxed in greater proportion than the less affluent. The least affluent of developed countries are rich, flushed with wealth as viewed by people of meaner states.

The perspective of the affluent dwellers is surprised to be included with the rich. Those that desire are never rich enough. Accumulation is a relentless endeavor that must be preserved against depletion. This world of our dwelling is multitudinous potential jealous of our time and effort. Riches and wealth are power that will dissipate without the vigil of those who would possess them. Greater wealth exerts an equal, greater pressure to escape containment. This circular condition does not readily release captives either.

Mat 4:8 Again, the devil taketh him up into an exceeding high mountain, and sheweth him all the kingdoms of the world, and the glory of them;
Mat 4:9 And saith unto him, All these things will I give thee, if thou wilt fall down and worship me.

Mar 10:22 And he was sad at that saying, and went away grieved: for he had great possessions.
Mar 10:23 And Jesus looked round about, and saith unto his disciples, How hardly shall they that have riches enter into the kingdom of God!
Mar 10:24 And the disciples were astonished at his words. But Jesus answereth again, and saith unto them, Children, how hard is it for them that trust in riches to enter into the kingdom of God!
Mar 10:25 It is easier for a camel to go through the eye of a needle, than for a rich man to enter into the kingdom of God.
Mar 10:26 And they were astonished out of measure, saying among themselves, Who then can be saved?
Mar 10:27 And Jesus looking upon them saith, with men [it is] impossible, but not with God: for with God all things are possible.
Mar 10:28 Then Peter began to say unto him, Lo, we have left all, and have followed thee.
Mar 10:29 And Jesus answered and said, Verily I say unto you, There is no man that hath left house, or

brethren, or sisters, or father, or mother, or wife, or
children, or lands, for my sake, and the gospel's,
Mar 10:30 But he shall receive an hundredfold now in
this time, houses, and brethren, and sisters, and
mothers, and children, and lands, with persecutions;
and in the world to come eternal life.
Mar 10:31 But many [that are] first shall be last; and
the last first.
And Mat 19:23 – 26, Luk 16:19 – 31

Luk 16:27 Then he said, I pray thee therefore, father,
that thou wouldest send him to my father's house:
Luk 16:28 For I have five brethren; that he may
testify unto them, lest they also come into this place
of torment.
Luk 16:29 Abraham saith unto him, They have Moses
and the prophets; let them hear them.
Luk 16:30 And he said, Nay, father Abraham: but if
one went unto them from the dead, they will repent.
Luk 16:31 And he said unto him, If they hear not
Moses and the prophets, neither will they be
persuaded, though one rose from the dead.

Jam 1:11 For the sun is no sooner risen with a burning
heat, but it withereth the grass, and the flower thereof
falleth, and the grace of the fashion of it perisheth: so
also shall the rich man fade away in his ways.

2Ti 4:1 I charge [thee] therefore before God, and the
Lord Jesus Christ, who shall judge the quick and the
dead at his appearing and his kingdom;
2Ti 4:2 Preach the word; be instant in season, out of
season; reprove, rebuke, exhort with all longsuffering
and doctrine.
2Ti 4:3 For the time will come when they will not
endure sound doctrine; but after their own lusts shall
they heap to themselves teachers, having itching ears;

2Ti 4:4 And they shall turn away [their] ears from the truth, and shall be turned unto fables.

Jhn 12:37 But though he had done so many miracles before them, yet they believed not on him:
Jhn 12:38 That the saying of Esaias the prophet might be fulfilled, which he spake, Lord, who hath believed our report? and to whom hath the arm of the Lord been revealed?
Jhn 12:39 Therefore they could not believe, because that Esaias said again,
Jhn 12:40 He hath blinded their eyes, and hardened their heart; that they should not see with [their] eyes, nor understand with [their] heart, and be converted, and I should heal them.
Jhn 12:41 These things said Esaias, when he saw his glory, and spake of him.
Jhn 12:42 Nevertheless among the chief rulers also many believed on him; but because of the Pharisees they did not confess [him], lest they should be put out of the synagogue:
Jhn 12:43 For they loved the praise of men more than the praise of God.
Jhn 12:44 Jesus cried and said, He that believeth on me, believeth not on me, but on him that sent me.
Jhn 12:45 And he that seeth me seeth him that sent me.

Pre flood humans lived their own versions of existence that had no place for their Creator.

Mat 24:37 But as the days of Noe [were], so shall also the coming of the Son of man be.
Mat 24:38 For as in the days that were before the flood they were eating and drinking, marrying and giving in marriage, until the day that Noe entered into the ark,

Mat 24:39 And knew not until the flood came, and took them all away; so shall also the coming of the Son of man be.
Mat 24:40 Then shall two be in the field; the one shall be taken, and the other left.
Mat 24:41 Two [women shall be] grinding at the mill; the one shall be taken, and the other left.
Mat 24:42 Watch therefore: for ye know not what hour your Lord doth come.
Mat 24:43 But know this, that if the goodman of the house had known in what watch the thief would come, he would have watched, and would not have suffered his house to be broken up.
Mat 24:44 Therefore be ye also ready: for in such an hour as ye think not the Son of man cometh.

Egyptians believed their existence was valid with invented gods and hierarchy wholly apart from their Creator.

Exd 7:3 And I will harden Pharaoh's heart, and multiply my signs and my wonders in the land of Egypt.
Exd 7:13 And he hardened Pharaoh's heart, that he hearkened not unto them; as the LORD had said.
Exd 7:14 And the LORD said unto Moses, Pharaoh's heart [is] hardened, he refuseth to let the people go.

Unbelief is ascendant today. This world disdains Jesus, the word of God. The end time table is prepared for the coming of the man of sin.

2Th 2:1 Now we beseech you, brethren, by the coming of our Lord Jesus Christ, and [by] our gathering together unto him,
2Th 2:2 That ye be not soon shaken in mind, or be troubled, neither by spirit, nor by word, nor by letter as from us, as that the day of Christ is at hand.

2Th 2:3 Let no man deceive you by any means: for [that day shall not come], except there come a falling away first, and that man of sin be revealed, the son of perdition;

2Th 2:4 Who opposeth and exalteth himself above all that is called God, or that is worshipped; so that he as God sitteth in the temple of God, shewing himself that he is God.

2Th 2:5 Remember ye not, that, when I was yet with you, I told you these things?

2Th 2:6 And now ye know what withholdeth that he might be revealed in his time.

2Th 2:7 For the mystery of iniquity doth already work: only he who now letteth [will let], until he be taken out of the way.

2Th 2:8 And then shall that Wicked be revealed, whom the Lord shall consume with the spirit of his mouth, and shall destroy with the brightness of his coming:

2Th 2:9 [Even him], whose coming is after the working of Satan with all power and signs and lying wonders,

2Th 2:10 And with all deceivableness of unrighteousness in them that perish; because they received not the love of the truth, that they might be saved.

2Th 2:11 And for this cause God shall send them strong delusion, that they should believe a lie:

2Th 2:12 That they all might be damned who believed not the truth, but had pleasure in unrighteousness.

2Th 2:13 But we are bound to give thanks alway to God for you, brethren beloved of the Lord, because God hath from the beginning chosen you to salvation through sanctification of the Spirit and belief of the truth:

2Th 2:14 Whereunto he called you by our gospel, to the obtaining of the glory of our Lord Jesus Christ.

2Th 2:15 Therefore, brethren, stand fast, and hold the traditions which ye have been taught, whether by word, or our epistle.
Psa 23:3 He restoreth my soul: he leadeth me in the paths of righteousness for his name's sake.
Psa 23:4 Yea, though I walk through the valley of the shadow of death, I will fear no evil: for thou [art] with me; thy rod and thy staff they comfort me.
Psa 23:5 Thou preparest a table before me in the presence of mine enemies: thou anointest my head with oil; my cup runneth over.
Psa 23:6 Surely goodness and mercy shall follow me all the days of my life: and I will dwell in the house of the LORD for ever.

Through the lens of a lifetime, neighboring your own life's span since the Scopes Trial of 1925 whose father is the Origin of Species published in 1859 this world is becoming more separated from the word of our Creator.

1Jo 4:2 Hereby know ye the Spirit of God: Every spirit that confesseth that Jesus Christ is come in the flesh is of God:
1Jo 4:3 And every spirit that confesseth not that Jesus Christ is come in the flesh is not of God: and this is that [spirit] of antichrist, whereof ye have heard that it should come; and even now already is it in the world.
1Jo 4:4 Ye are of God, little children, and have overcome them: because greater is he that is in you, than he that is in the world.
1Jo 4:5 They are of the world: therefore speak they of the world, and the world heareth them.

God created humanity for His glory and God knows the future. In the Garden of Eden God paused, knowing the entirety of the human spectacle for all time, to show Adam and Eve's condition just after their sin. God paused for us.

Jhn 12:28 Father, glorify thy name. Then came there a voice from heaven, [saying], I have both glorified [it], and will glorify [it] again.
Jhn 12:29 The people therefore, that stood by, and heard [it], said that it thundered: others said, An angel spake to Him.
Jhn 12:30 Jesus answered and said, This voice came not because of Me, but for your sakes.

Genesis, true to the recurrent manner of biblical focus, now proceeds to further illustrate and emphasize the seed of God's grace for humanity. At the 11th chapter Abraham is born of the lineage of Seth. The life of Abraham is followed over 13 chapters of Genesis. Leading into the 11th chapter, God proclaimed the consequences of disobedience. Adam and Eve disobeyed and their children are born in that likeness producing fruit with the knowledge of good and evil. The lineage of Cain was briefly followed to confirm humanity's fate without God. In faith Noah, the 8th generation of Seth, believed God to preserve a remnant of humanity from the purging of the sinful generations.

Hbr 11:7 By faith Noah, being warned of God of things not seen as yet, moved with fear, prepared an ark to the saving of his house; by the which he condemned the world, and became heir of the righteousness which is by faith.

God is perfect. His gifts are sure. He does not defend His Word. God is truth. He does not prevent the consequences of anyone determined to contradict truth because they will fail. Clearly, there is but one hope for deliverance as revealed in faithful Noah and now reaffirmed in Abraham. Deliverance will not come from human effort without God. In Genesis and all the word of God, obedience is not forced. God even pleads with His children to choose life. There is always room for repentance until judgment. God will forgive us every time we ask.

1Jo 1:9 If we confess our sins, he is faithful and just to forgive us [our] sins, and to cleanse us from all unrighteousness.

2Pe 3:15 And account [that] the longsuffering of our Lord [is] salvation; even as our beloved brother Paul also according to the wisdom given unto him hath written unto you;
Eze 33:11 Say unto them, [As] I live, saith the Lord GOD, I have no pleasure in the death of the wicked; but that the wicked turn from his way and live: turn ye, turn ye from your evil ways; for why will ye die, O house of Israel?
Eze 33:12 Therefore, thou son of man, say unto the children of thy people, The righteousness of the righteous shall not deliver him in the day of his transgression: as for the wickedness of the wicked, he shall not fall thereby in the day that he turneth from his wickedness; neither shall the righteous be able to live for his [righteousness] in the day that he sinneth.
Eze 33:13 When I shall say to the righteous, [that] he shall surely live; if he trust to his own righteousness, and commit iniquity, all his righteousnesses shall not be remembered; but for his iniquity that he hath committed, he shall die for it.
Eze 33:14 Again, when I say unto the wicked, Thou shalt surely die; if he turn from his sin, and do that which is lawful and right;
Eze 33:15 [If] the wicked restore the pledge, give again that he had robbed, walk in the statutes of life, without committing iniquity; he shall surely live, he shall not die.

Eze 33:16 None of his sins that he hath committed shall be mentioned unto him: he hath done that which is lawful and right; he shall surely live.
Eze 33:17 Yet the children of thy people say, The way of the Lord is not equal: but as for them, their way is not equal.
Eze 33:18 When the righteous turneth from his righteousness, and committeth iniquity, he shall even die thereby.
Eze 33:19 But if the wicked turn from his wickedness, and do that which is lawful and right, he shall live thereby.
Eze 33:20 Yet ye say, The way of the Lord is not equal. O ye house of Israel, I will judge you every one after his ways.
Rom 12:21 Be not overcome of evil, but overcome evil with good.

Hope for humanity is displayed in the pre flood era as men begin to call upon the name of the Lord. Apparently calling upon the name of the Lord is a change. Whatever else is to be known from this statement men call upon the name of the Lord Who they believe and acknowledge. Noah exhibits the fruit of those who call upon the name of the Lord and then in Abraham faith is more fully known.

Gen 4:25 And Adam knew his wife again; and she bare a son, and called his name Seth: For God, [said she], hath appointed me another seed instead of Abel, whom Cain slew.
Gen 4:26 And to Seth, to him also there was born a son; and he called his name Enos: then began men to call upon the name of the LORD.
Rom 4:3 For what saith the scripture? Abraham believed God, and it was counted unto him for righteousness.

Rom 4:16 Therefore [it is] of faith, that [it might be] by grace; to the end the promise might be sure to all the seed; not to that only which is of the law, but to that also which is of the faith of Abraham; who is the father of us all,
Gal 3:6 Even as Abraham believed God, and it was accounted to him for righteousness.
Rom 10:11 For the scripture saith, Whosoever believeth on him shall not be ashamed.
Rom 10:12 For there is no difference between the Jew and the Greek: for the same Lord over all is rich unto all that call upon him.
Jam 2:23 And the scripture was fulfilled which saith, Abraham believed God, and it was imputed unto him for righteousness: and he was called the Friend of God.

Gen 18:19 For I know him, that he will command his children and his household after him, and they shall keep the way of the LORD, to do justice and judgment; that the LORD may bring upon Abraham that which he hath spoken of him.

Unto Abraham

Creation is more detailed in the second chapter of Genesis and in the fourth chapter the last mention of Cain's murdering lineage has description absent since Cain. The Genesis method of revelation, to more fully display the results of behavior after and until it is evidenced by the subject's actions is called out and due by the tragic course of the first 11 chapters. Genesis redeems faith as Noah heeds God to prepare the vessel; then Abraham believes God Who provides a son from a dead womb and the altar of sacrifice in condemnation of unbelief through this champion of faith. The challenge to validity, the indifference, temptation, rejection and contention, the tragedy of human focus apart from God is exercised by choice for the greater part of humanity from the first through to the end of the human controversy. The bible history relates idolatry, slavery, murder and wars that evidence wickedness greater than the subject persons and peoples. Theory and explanation of human existence apart from the brutality and manipulation documented in human history cannot dismiss these events as merely a brief moment in the entirety of human existence. Belief in God weaves through Seth's lineage to Noah, is not remarkable in the post flood repopulation of Earth and then is contrasted with Abraham.

Abram is born, marries Sarai and moves with his father to a different city, Haran, at the end of chapter 11. The biblical display of the concept of faith through Abram\Abraham is witnessed in the first decision of his own apart from that of his father. What is to be known through Abraham begins with the very first verse of chapter 12.

Gen 12:1 Now the LORD had said unto Abram, Get thee out of thy country, and from thy kindred, and from thy father's house, unto a land that I will shew thee:

God knows that Abram will follow His instructions as He directs, absent of indecision to depart from his native land and all the support that accrues with community. The introduction to the display of Abram\Abraham's choices is faith in God.

God next declares that He begins with Abram that which human effort cannot produce. Against the sorry example of the human experience since Adam and Eve, God makes seven promises to\through Abram. God begins the redemption of humans.

Gen 12:2 And I will make of thee a great nation, and I will bless thee, and make thy name great; and thou shalt be a blessing:

Gen 12:3 And I will bless them that bless thee, and curse him that curseth thee: and in thee shall all families of the earth be blessed.

Abram's first choice after the death of his father is to faithfully leave his home, obedient to God's direction.

Gen 12:4 So Abram departed, as the LORD had spoken unto him; and Lot went with him: and Abram [was] seventy and five years old when he departed out of Haran.
Gen 12:5 And Abram took Sarai his wife, and Lot his brother's son, and all their substance that they had gathered, and the souls that they had gotten in Haran; and they went forth to go into the land of Canaan; and into the land of Canaan they came.
Gen 12:6 And Abram passed through the land unto the place of Sichem, unto the plain of Moreh. And the Canaanite [was] then in the land.
Gen 12:7 And the LORD appeared unto Abram, and said, Unto thy seed will I give this land: and there builded he an altar unto the LORD, who appeared unto him.

Hbr 11:8 By faith Abraham, when he was called to go out into a place which he should after receive for an inheritance, obeyed; and he went out, not knowing whither he went.
Hbr 11:10 For he looked for a city which hath foundations, whose builder and maker [is] God.
Hbr 11:15 And truly, if they had been mindful of that [country] from whence they came out, they might have had opportunity to have returned.
Hbr 11:16 But now they desire a better [country], that is, an heavenly:wherefore God is not ashamed to be called their God: for he hath prepared for them a city.

Chapter 9
Our Focus

Consider the description of Lucifer and yet the bible does not state that he was created in the image of God. Satan recognizes this in his determination to destroy human kind. Would not the beings created in the image of God be an expression of His Spirit? God, His Spirit was not fully comprehended and too soon forfeited. The lost presence of God waits in tension throughout the Old Testament until in the fullness of time God restores the potential to reunite with His Spirit, with Him. Spirit of utter value must not be wasted again. God only inhabits those who choose Him, which choice is only available because of redemption.

Gal 4:4 But when the fulness of the time was come, God sent forth his Son, made of a woman, made under the law,
Col 1:27 To whom God would make known what [is] the riches of the glory of this mystery among the Gentiles; which is Christ in you, the hope of glory:
Mat 5:5 Blessed [are] the meek: for they shall inherit the earth.
Mat 11:29 Take my yoke upon you, and learn of me; for I am meek and lowly in heart: and ye shall find rest unto your souls.
1Cr 13:4 Charity suffereth long, [and] is kind; charity envieth not; charity vaunteth not itself, is not puffed up,
1Cr 13:5 Doth not behave itself unseemly, seeketh not her own, is not easily provoked, thinketh no evil;
1Cr 13:6 Rejoiceth not in iniquity, but rejoiceth in the truth;
1Cr 13:7 Beareth all things, believeth all things, hopeth all things, endureth all things.
Psa 34:8 O taste and see that the LORD [is] good: blessed [is] the man [that] trusteth in him.

Mat 19:17 And he said unto him, Why callest thou me good? [there is] none good but one, [that is], God: but if thou wilt enter into life, keep the commandments.

Mat 19:25 When his disciples heard [it], they were exceedingly amazed, saying, Who then can be saved?

Mat 19:26 But Jesus beheld [them], and said unto them, With men this is impossible; but with God all things are possible.

Mar 10:18 And Jesus said unto him, Why callest thou me good? [there is] none good but one, [that is], God.

Mar 10:26 And they were astonished out of measure, saying among themselves, Who then can be saved?

Mar 10:27 And Jesus looking upon them saith, With men [it is] impossible, but not with God: for with God all things are possible.

Luk 18:19 And Jesus said unto him, Why callest thou me good? none [is] good, save one, [that is], God.

Luk 18:26 And they that heard [it] said, Who then can be saved?

Luk 18:27 And he said, The things which are impossible with men are possible with God.

Jhn 8:34 Jesus answered them, Verily, verily, I say unto you, Whosoever committeth sin is the servant of sin.

Jhn 5:30 I can of mine own self do nothing: as I hear, I judge: and my judgment is just; because I seek not mine own will, but the will of the Father which hath sent me.

Jhn 8:29 And he that sent me is with me: the Father hath not left me alone; for I do always those things that please him.

Jhn 12:49 For I have not spoken of myself; but the Father which sent me, he gave me a commandment, what I should say, and what I should speak.

Jhn 14:24 He that loveth me not keepeth not my sayings: and the word which ye hear is not mine, but the Father's which sent me.

Psa 104:31 The glory of the LORD shall endure for ever: the LORD shall rejoice in his works.
Psa 104:32 He looketh on the earth, and it trembleth: he toucheth the hills, and they smoke.
Psa 104:33 I will sing unto the LORD as long as I live: I will sing praise to my God while I have my being.
Psa 104:34 My meditation of him shall be sweet: I will be glad in the LORD.
Psa 104:35 Let the sinners be consumed out of the earth, and let the wicked be no more. Bless thou the LORD, O my soul. Praise ye the LORD.

Fruit of the tree of the knowledge of good and evil awakened in humans a knowledge of self and the consequences of such. None will claim self-ish-ness is their preferred conduct but the human spectacle of Genesis, excepting few examples, is selfish driven tragedy. There are other words descriptive of this fruit. Betrayal, false, gainsay, heresy, murder, supplant or theft are all fruits of selfishness. Adam and Eve's disobedience chose personal desire discounting the warning of a loving father.

Gen 3:1 Now the serpent was more subtil than any beast of the field which the LORD God had made. And he said unto the woman, Yea, hath God said, Ye shall not eat of every tree of the garden?
Gen 3:2 And the woman said unto the serpent, We may eat of the fruit of the trees of the garden:
Gen 3:3 But of the fruit of the tree which [is] in the midst of the garden, God hath said, Ye shall not eat of it, neither shall ye touch it, lest ye die.
Gen 3:4 And the serpent said unto the woman, Ye shall not surely die:

Gen 3:5 For God doth know that in the day ye eat thereof, then your eyes shall be opened, and ye shall be as gods, knowing good and evil.
Gen 3:6 And when the woman saw that the tree [was] good for food, and that it [was] pleasant to the eyes, and a tree to be desired to make [one] wise, she took of the fruit thereof, and did eat, and gave also unto her husband with her; and he did eat.
Gen 3:7 And the eyes of them both were opened, and they knew that they [were] naked; and they sewed fig leaves together, and made themselves aprons.

Gal 5:17 For the flesh lusteth against the Spirit, and the Spirit against the flesh: and these are contrary the one to the other: so that ye cannot do the things that ye would.
Mat 6:24 No man can serve two masters: for either he will hate the one, and love the other; or else he will hold to the one, and despise the other. Ye cannot serve God and mammon. Also Luke 16:13
Mat 21:28 But what think ye? A [certain] man had two sons; and he came to the first, and said, Son, go work to day in my vineyard.
Mat 21:29 He answered and said, I will not: but afterward he repented, and went.
Mat 21:30 And he came to the second, and said likewise. And he answered and said, I [go], sir: and went not.
Mat 21:31 Whether of them twain did the will of [his] father? They say unto him, The first. Jesus saith unto them, Verily I say unto you, That the publicans and the harlots go into the kingdom of God before you.

God is not ashamed

Redemption that humans can never attain through their own efforts since the offended is God and the offense resides in the flesh, is offered in lovingkindness, tender mercy and empowering grace. God does not force obedience. God is patient, He suffers the disappointments, the offenses from His children, He is faithful and constant, the very source of truth. God is not ashamed to be called God by those who choose Him.

Eph 4:24 And that ye put on the new man, which after God is created in righteousness and true holiness.
Col 3:10 And have put on the new [man], which is renewed in knowledge after the image of him that created him:
Jhn 3:6 That which is born of the flesh is flesh; and that which is born of the Spirit is spirit.
Jhn 3:7 Marvel not that I said unto thee, Ye must be born again.
2Cr 3:18 But we all, with open face beholding as in a glass the glory of the Lord, are changed into the same image from glory to glory, [even] as by the Spirit of the Lord.
2Cr 4:6 For God, who commanded the light to shine out of darkness, hath shined in our hearts, to [give] the light of the knowledge of the glory of God in the face of Jesus Christ.
Psalm 40
Exd 34:6 And the LORD passed by before him, and proclaimed, The LORD, The LORD God, merciful and gracious, longsuffering, and abundant in goodness and truth,
Hbr 11:16 But now they desire a better [country], that is, an heavenly: wherefore God is not ashamed to be called their God: for he hath prepared for them a city.

Your Choice

Mat 8:13 And Jesus said unto the centurion, Go thy way; and as thou hast believed, [so] be it done unto thee. And his servant was healed in the selfsame hour.
Mat 9:29 Then touched he their eyes, saying, According to your faith be it unto you.
Luk 19:22 And he saith unto him, Out of thine own mouth will I judge thee, [thou] wicked servant. Thou knewest that I was an austere man, taking up that I laid not down, and reaping that I did not sow:
Mat 6:22 The light of the body is the eye: if therefore thine eye be single, thy whole body shall be full of light.
Mat 6:23 But if thine eye be evil, thy whole body shall be full of darkness. If therefore the light that is in thee be darkness, how great [is] that darkness!

Jos 24:14 now therefore fear the LORD, and serve him in sincerity and in truth: and put away the gods which your fathers served on the other side of the flood, and in Egypt; and serve ye the LORD.
Jos 24:15 And if it seem evil unto you to serve the LORD, choose you this day whom ye will serve; whether the gods which your fathers served that [were] on the other side of the flood, or the gods of the Amorites, in whose land ye dwell: but as for me and my house, we will serve the LORD.

Jam 2:23 And the scripture was fulfilled which saith, Abraham believed God, and it was imputed unto him for righteousness: and he was called the Friend of God.
Also Rom 4:3, Gal 3:6
2Pe 2:4 For if God spared not the angels that sinned, but cast [them] down to hell, and delivered [them]

into chains of darkness, to be reserved unto judgment;
2Pe 2:5 And spared not the old world, but saved Noah the eighth [person], a preacher of righteousness, bringing in the flood upon the world of the ungodly;
2Pe 2:6 And turning the cities of Sodom and Gomorrha into ashes condemned [them] with an overthrow, making [them] an ensample unto those that after should live ungodly;
2Pe 2:7 And delivered just Lot, vexed with the filthy conversation of the wicked:
2Pe 2:8 (For that righteous man dwelling among them, in seeing and hearing, vexed [his] righteous soul from day to day with [their] unlawful deeds;)
2Pe 2:9 The Lord knoweth how to deliver the godly out of temptations, and to reserve the unjust unto the day of judgment to be punished:
Jud 1:16 These are murmurers, complainers, walking after their own lusts; and their mouth speaketh great swelling [words], having men's persons in admiration because of advantage.
Jud 1:17 But, beloved, remember ye the words which were spoken before of the apostles of our Lord Jesus Christ;
Jud 1:18 How that they told you there should be mockers in the last time, who should walk after their own ungodly lusts.
Jud 1:19These be they who separate themselves, sensual, having not the Spirit.
Jud 1:20 But ye, beloved, building up yourselves on your most holy faith, praying in the Holy Ghost,
Jud 1:21 Keep yourselves in the love of God, looking for the mercy of our Lord Jesus Christ unto eternal life.
Jud 1:22 And of some have compassion, making a difference:

Jud 1:23 And others save with fear, pulling [them] out of the fire; hating even the garment spotted by the flesh.
Jud 1:24 Now unto him that is able to keep you from falling, and to present [you] faultless before the presence of his glory with exceeding joy,
Jud 1:25 To the only wise God our Saviour, [be] glory and majesty, dominion and power, both now and ever. Amen.

Your Heart

The reality of human being is undergirded by thought. Truly, choice is the expression of our existence. Our choices place us where we are in a geographical location but more to the point, who we are, our person is self made. All of us have frequently been at the moment of decision when activity stops, is suspended and reserved in potential, it is very human. Humanity is participating in creation. Human life is more than animal interaction with the environment; it is an expression of beliefs. How very conscious, how precious is the ability to choose. What a perfect gift is the life that chooses to believe God. The honor, the glory due the creator then resides where it belongs. The human spectacle witnesses instead a majority of lives apart from the counsel of God.

Luk 12:34 For where your treasure is, there will your heart be also.
1Jo 2:17 And the world passeth away, and the lust thereof: but he that doeth the will of God abideth for ever.
2Ti 1:1 Paul, an apostle of Jesus Christ by the will of God, according to the promise of life which is in Christ Jesus,

God is True

Jam 1:18 Of His own will begat He us with the word of truth, that we should be a kind of firstfruits of His creatures.

Isa 45:23 I have sworn by Myself, the word is gone out of My mouth [in] righteousness, and shall not return, That unto Me every knee shall bow, every tongue shall swear.

Isa 55:11 So shall My word be that goeth forth out of My mouth: it shall not return unto Me void, but it shall accomplish that which I please, and it shall prosper [in the thing] whereto I sent it.

Eze 12:25 For I [am] the LORD: I will speak, and the word that I shall speak shall come to pass; it shall be no more prolonged: for in your days, O rebellious house, will I say the word, and will perform it, saith the Lord GOD.

Eze 12:26 Again the word of the LORD came to me, saying,

Eze 12:27 Son of man, behold, [they of] the house of Israel say, the vision that he seeth [is] for many days [to come], and he prophesieth of the times [that are] far off.

Eze 12:28 Therefore say unto them, Thus saith the Lord GOD; There shall none of my words be prolonged any more, but the word which I have spoken shall be done, saith the Lord GOD.

Zec 4:6 Then he answered and spake unto me, saying, This [is] the word of the LORD unto Zerubbabel, saying, Not by might, nor by power, but by my spirit, saith the LORD of hosts.

Mat 3:13 Then cometh Jesus from Galilee to Jordan unto John, to be baptized of him.

Mat 3:14 But John forbad him, saying, I have need to be baptized of thee, and comest thou to me?

Mat 3:15 And Jesus answering said unto him, Suffer [it to be so] now: for thus it becometh us to fulfill all righteousness. Then he suffered him.

Mat 3:16 And Jesus, when he was baptized, went up straightway out of the water: and, lo, the heavens were opened unto him, and he saw the Spirit of God descending like a dove, and lighting upon him:

Mat 3:17 And lo a voice from heaven, saying, This is my beloved Son, in whom I am well pleased.

Mat 4:1 Then was Jesus led up of the Spirit into the wilderness to be tempted of the devil.

Mar 1:7 And preached, saying, There cometh one mightier than I after me, the latchet of whose shoes I am not worthy to stoop down and unloose.

Mar 1:8 I indeed have baptized you with water: but he shall baptize you with the Holy Ghost.

Mar 1:9 And it came to pass in those days, that Jesus came from Nazareth of Galilee, and was baptized of John in Jordan.

Mar 1:10 And straightway coming up out of the water, he saw the heavens opened, and the Spirit like a dove descending upon him:

Mar 1:11 And there came a voice from heaven, [saying], Thou art my beloved Son, in whom I am well pleased.

Mar 1:12 And immediately the Spirit driveth him into the wilderness.

Mar 1:13 And he was there in the wilderness forty days, tempted of Satan; and was with the wild beasts; and the angels ministered unto him.

Luk 4:14 And Jesus returned in the power of the Spirit into Galilee: and there went out a fame of him through all the region round about.

Luk 4:18 The Spirit of the Lord [is] upon me, because He hath anointed me to preach the gospel to the poor;

He hath sent me to heal the brokenhearted, to preach deliverance to the captives, and recovering of sight to the blind, to set at liberty them that are bruised,
Mar 1:14 Now after that John was put in prison, Jesus came into Galilee, preaching the gospel of the kingdom of God,
Mar 1:15 And saying, The time is fulfilled, and the kingdom of God is at hand: repent ye, and believe the gospel.

The Spirit, to know the mysteries of the Kingdom of God

Mat 13:11 He answered and said unto them, Because it is given unto you to know the mysteries of the kingdom of heaven, but to them it is not given.
Mat 13:35 That it might be fulfilled which was spoken by the prophet, saying, I will open my mouth in parables; I will utter things which have been kept secret from the foundation of the world.
Luk 8:10 And he said, Unto you it is given to know the mysteries of the kingdom of God: but to others in parables; that seeing they might not see, and hearing they might not understand.
Hsa 4:6 My people are destroyed for lack of knowledge: because thou hast rejected knowledge, I will also reject thee, that thou shalt be no priest to me: seeing thou hast forgotten the law of thy God, I will also forget thy children.
Jhn 3:10 Jesus answered and said unto him, Art thou a master of Israel, and knowest not these things?
Pro 14:12 There is a way which seemeth right unto a man, but the end thereof [are] the ways of death.

The hidden knowledge and mysteries of God are opened to the understanding of the spiritual, those who are born again. God formed man of the dust of the ground and breathed the breath of life into him.   Humanity lost the Spirit of God by partaking of the forbidden fruit. Jesus breathed on the apostles and said to them, "Receive ye the Holy Ghost." (Jhn 20:22). Jesus declares "you must be born again". (Jhn 3:7) This rebirth is not optional but "must" occur.

Gen 2:7 And the LORD God formed man [of] the dust of the ground, and breathed into his nostrils the breath of life; and man became a living soul.
Jhn 20:22 And when he had said this, he breathed on [them], and saith unto them, Receive ye the Holy Ghost:
Luk 3:16 John answered, saying unto [them] all, I indeed baptize you with water; but one mightier than I cometh, the latchet of whose shoes I am not worthy to unloose: he shall baptize you with the Holy Ghost and with fire:
Luk 3:17 Whose fan [is] in his hand, and he will throughly purge his floor, and will gather the wheat into his garner; but the chaff he will burn with fire unquenchable.
1Cr 15:45 And so it is written, The first man Adam was made a living soul; the last Adam [was made] a quickening spirit.
1Cr 15:46 Howbeit that [was] not first which is spiritual, but that which is natural; and afterward that which is spiritual.
1Cr 15:47 The first man [is] of the earth, earthy: the second man [is] the Lord from heaven.

1Cr 2:10 But God hath revealed [them] unto us by his Spirit: for the Spirit searcheth all things, yea, the deep things of God.
1Cr 2:11 For what man knoweth the things of a man, save the spirit of man which is in him? even so the things of God knoweth no man, but the Spirit of God.

1Cr 2:12 Now we have received, not the spirit of the world, but the Spirit which is of God; that we might know the things that are freely given to us of God.
1Cr 2:13 Which things also we speak, not in the words which man's wisdom teacheth, but which the Holy Ghost teacheth; comparing spiritual things with spiritual.
1Cr 2:14 But the natural man receiveth not the things of the Spirit of God: for they are foolishness unto him: neither can he know [them], because they are spiritually discerned.

To what purpose is this fragile gift of life? This is the question most deserving of intense scrutiny. Is there truly an answer for life, for who we are? The history of humanity folds back and forth to the same end. As we tread on our ancestors our question should be, shall we wait for several thousands of years to possibly evolve further? There is no middle ground or comfortable agreement, no truce is possible for the 2 opposing scenarios of creation. The gradual, thoughtless development of life contradicts a creator who chooses to cause human being. The purpose for life is absent in one of these competing contexts intent or happenstance. Is human being simply an intricate receptor of feeling? The concept of God, the supernatural being is the actual contention. The wisdom of God in a mystery, the hidden wisdom is not discernible by the natural man who relies on the wisdom of this world. Study and contemplate His promise and description of who we truly are. God, the Creator is inconceivably personal to the deepest most internal mote of being.

1Cr 2:5 That your faith should not stand in the wisdom of men, but in the power of God.
1Cr 2:6 Howbeit we speak wisdom among them that are perfect: yet not the wisdom of this world, nor of the princes of this world, that come to nought:

1Cr 2:7 But we speak the wisdom of God in a mystery, [even] the hidden [wisdom], which God ordained before the world unto our glory:

1Cr 2:8 Which none of the princes of this world knew: for had they known [it], they would not have crucified the Lord of glory.

Luk 24:49 And, behold, I send the promise of my Father upon you: but tarry ye in the city of Jerusalem, until ye be endued with power from on high.

Act 1:4 And, being assembled together with [them], commanded them that they should not depart from Jerusalem, but wait for the promise of the Father, which, [saith he], ye have heard of me.

Jhn 14:16 And I will pray the Father, and he shall give you another Comforter, that he may abide with you for ever;

Jhn 14:17[Even] the Spirit of truth; whom the world cannot receive, because it seeth him not, neither knoweth him: but ye know him; for he dwelleth with you, and shall be in you.

Jhn 14:18 I will not leave you comfortless: I will come to you.

Mar 4:11 And He said unto them, Unto you it is given to know the mystery of the kingdom of God: but unto them that are without, all [these] things are done in parables:

Mat 6:33 But seek ye first the kingdom of God, and His righteousness; and all these things shall be added unto you.

Mar 10:15 Verily I say unto you, Whosoever shall not receive the kingdom of God as a little child, he shall not enter therein.

Mar 10:24 And the disciples were astonished at his words. But Jesus answereth again, and saith unto them, Children, how hard is it for them that trust in riches to enter into the kingdom of God!

Luk 13:18 Then said He, Unto what is the kingdom of God like? and whereunto shall I resemble it?

Luk 13:19 It is like a grain of mustard seed, which a man took, and cast into his garden; and it grew, and waxed a great tree; and the fowls of the air lodged in the branches of it.

Luk 13:20 And again He said, Whereunto shall I liken the kingdom of God?

Luk 13:21 It is like leaven, which a woman took and hid in three measures of meal, till the whole was leavened.

Luk 17:20 And when He was demanded of the Pharisees, when the kingdom of God should come, He answered them and said, The kingdom of God cometh not with observation:

Luk 17:21 Neither shall they say, Lo here! or, lo there! for, behold, the kingdom of God is within you.

Jhn 3:3 Jesus answered and said unto him, Verily, verily, I say unto thee, Except a man be born again, he cannot see the kingdom of God.

Jhn 3:5 Jesus answered, Verily, verily, I say unto thee, Except a man be born of water and [of] the Spirit, he cannot enter into the kingdom of God.

Rom 14:17 For the kingdom of God is not meat and drink; but righteousness, and peace, and joy in the Holy Ghost.

1Cr 4:20 For the kingdom of God [is] not in word, but in power.

Num 14:21 But [as] truly [as] I live, all the earth shall be filled with the glory of the LORD.

Hab 2:14 For the earth shall be filled with the knowledge of the glory of the LORD, as the waters cover the sea.

2Pe 3:13 Nevertheless we, according to His promise, look for new heavens and a new earth, wherein dwelleth righteousness.

Rev 21:3 And I heard a great voice out of heaven saying, Behold, the tabernacle of God [is] with men, and He will dwell with them, and they shall be His people, and God Himself shall be with them, [and be] their God.

Mat 6:10 Thy kingdom come. Thy will be done in earth, as [it is] in heaven.

Rom 13:11 And that, knowing the time, that now [it is] high time to awake out of sleep: for now [is] our salvation nearer than when we believed.

Rom 13:12 The night is far spent, the day is at hand: let us therefore cast off the works of darkness, and let us put on the armour of light.

Rom 13:13 Let us walk honestly, as in the day; not in rioting and drunkenness, not in chambering and wantonness, not in strife and envying.

Rom 13:14 But put ye on the Lord Jesus Christ, and make not provision for the flesh, to [fulfil] the lusts [thereof].

Small Review

Genesis, choice:
1. God chooses to speak creation
2. God, the Creator warns Adam
3. Man and woman are family of God
4. Cunning and intrigue violate the word of God
5. Choice severs the Spirit of God
6. Adam and Eve know (hide from the truth, hide from God)
7. Focus on Who, self-ish-ness
8. Potent, Revitalizing Tree of Life is denied to sin
9. Consequences of sin, corruption apart from the Spirit of God
10. Sin, a most fertile seed survives flood cleansed earth
11. Human choice is not aligned with God
12. Believe God, Only God can Redeem, the Lamb of God
13. The offended, denied, rejected is God

14. God is a spirit, choose the will of God, Receive the Spirit
15. Account the lease of life, Judgment

Tree, whose seed is in itself, yields fruits, according to its kind, upon the earth

Our seed; is it of the flesh or of the spirit? Our choices determine Who and What We Are, our fruit. Our personal choices, our life upon the earth produce fruit that influence those of our cohabitation. The spirit creates life. The flesh consumes. God is not willing that any should perish.

2Pe 3:9 The Lord is not slack concerning his promise, as some men count slackness; but is longsuffering to us-ward, not willing that any should perish, but that all should come to repentance.
1Jo 2:17 And the world passeth away, and the lust thereof: but he that doeth the will of God abideth for ever.
Jhn 8:29 And he that sent me is with me: the Father hath not left me alone; for I do always those things that please him.
Eph 1:1 Paul, an apostle of Jesus Christ by the will of God, to the saints which are at Ephesus, and to the faithful in Christ Jesus:
Jhn 3:15 That whosoever believeth in him should not perish, but have eternal life.
Jhn 3:16 For God so loved the world, that he gave his only begotten Son, that whosoever believeth in him should not perish, but have everlasting life.
Rom 8:8 So then they that are in the flesh cannot please God.
Gal 6:8 For he that soweth to his flesh shall of the flesh reap corruption; but he that soweth to the Spirit shall of the Spirit reap life everlasting.

Mat 7:13 Enter ye in at the strait gate: for wide [is] the gate, and broad [is] the way, that leadeth to destruction, and many there be which go in thereat:

Mat 7:14 Because strait [is] the gate, and narrow [is] the way, which leadeth unto life, and few there be that find it.

Mat 7:15 Beware of false prophets, which come to you in sheep's clothing, but inwardly they are ravening wolves.

Mat 7:16 Ye shall know them by their fruits. Do men gather grapes of thorns, or figs of thistles?

Mat 7:17 Even so every good tree bringeth forth good fruit; but a corrupt tree bringeth forth evil fruit.

Mat 7:18 A good tree cannot bring forth evil fruit, neither [can] a corrupt tree bring forth good fruit.

Mat 7:19 Every tree that bringeth not forth good fruit is hewn down, and cast into the fire.

Mat 7:20 Wherefore by their fruits ye shall know them.

Mat 7:21 Not every one that saith unto me, Lord, Lord, shall enter into the kingdom of heaven; but he that doeth the will of my Father which is in heaven.

Mat 7:22 Many will say to me in that day, Lord, Lord, have we not prophesied in thy name? and in thy name have cast out devils? and in thy name done many wonderful works?

Mat 7:23 And then will I profess unto them, I never knew you: depart from me, ye that work iniquity.

Rom 8:14 For as many as are led by the Spirit of God, they are the sons of God.

Rom 8:16 The Spirit itself beareth witness with our spirit, that we are the children of God:

Rom 12:2 And be not conformed to this world: but be ye transformed by the renewing of your mind, that ye may prove what [is] that good, and acceptable, and perfect, will of God.

1Cr 15:46 Howbeit that [was] not first which is spiritual, but that which is natural; and afterward that which is spiritual.

The Spirit of God is lost to humanity in disobedience verifying the strength of desire and affirms the subtle serpent's intention. Consider how we know of war, mutilation, torture, dungeons, famine, plunder, beheading, rape, incest, disembowelment and too many other descriptions of rampant evil committed by humans all of which are shockingly horrific merely to be listed. Undoubtedly success on this scale is not a chance trigger but reveals the intensity and panorama of thought committed to challenge and corruption. The archfiend, Satan, is contending God, who and what He is and disdains prophecy of his own defeat as mere propaganda but becomes savagely desperate as the end to the human creation process nears. Satan's judgment ultimately is confirmed in the beings he disdained.

Satan has confirmation of willfulness and ruin in wars. Man has conducted wars of finance to subjugate other peoples, has planned famines to conduct wars of starvation, is conducting intense research to develop wars of diseases and has harnessed the atom to melt flesh and buildings or, with more precision to eliminate only the living, thus preserving more valuable buildings. Satan must be encouraged by people who license murder of the innocent passing laws that entrap their opponents or slay the unborn. Humans are focused on the physical and we desire and are preoccupied with everything but God's will.

Gen 6:5 And GOD saw that the wickedness of man [was] great in the earth, and [that] every imagination of the thoughts of his heart [was] only evil continually. Gen 6:6 And it repented the LORD that he had made man on the earth, and it grieved him at his heart.

Jer 17:9 The heart [is] deceitful above all [things], and desperately wicked: who can know it?

Jer 17:10 I the LORD search the heart, [I] try the reins, even to give every man according to his ways, [and] according to the fruit of his doings.

2Ti 3:1 this know also, that in the last days perilous times shall come.

2Ti 3:2 for men shall be lovers of their own selves, covetous, boasters, proud, blasphemers, disobedient to parents, unthankful, unholy,

2Ti 3:3 without natural affection, trucebreakers, false accusers, incontinent, fierce, despisers of those that are good,

2Ti 3:4 Traitors, heady, highminded, lovers of pleasures more than lovers of God;

2Ti 3:5 Having a form of godliness, but denying the power thereof: from such turn away.

2Ti 3:6 For of this sort are they which creep into houses, and lead captive silly women laden with sins, led away with divers lusts,

2Ti 3:7 Ever learning, and never able to come to the knowledge of the truth.

Rom 2:19 And art confident that thou thyself art a guide of the blind, a light of them which are in darkness,

2Pe 1:9 But he that lacketh these things is blind, and cannot see afar off, and hath forgotten that he was purged from his old sins.

Rev 3:17 Because thou sayest, I am rich, and increased with goods, and have need of nothing; and knowest not that thou art wretched, and miserable, and poor, and blind, and naked:

Luk 24:44 and he said unto them, These [are] the words which I spake unto you, while I was yet with you, that all things must be fulfilled, which were written in the law of Moses, and [in] the prophets, and [in] the psalms, concerning me.

Luk 24:45 Then opened he their understanding, that they might understand the scriptures,

Luk 24:46 And said unto them, Thus it is written, and thus it behoved Christ to suffer, and to rise from the dead the third day:

Luk 24:47 And that repentance and remission of sins should be preached in his name among all nations, beginning at Jerusalem.

Luk 24:48 And ye are witnesses of these things.

Luk 24:49 And, behold, I send the promise of my Father upon you: but tarry ye in the city of Jerusalem, until ye be endued with power from on high.

Hbr 4:14 Seeing then that we have a great high priest, that is passed into the heavens, Jesus the Son of God, let us hold fast [our] profession.

Hbr 4:15 For we have not an high priest which cannot be touched with the feeling of our infirmities; but was in all points tempted like as [we are, yet] without sin.

Hbr 4:16 Let us therefore come boldly unto the throne of grace, that we may obtain mercy, and find grace to help in time of need

2Cr 5:14 For the love of Christ constraineth us; because we thus judge, that if one died for all, then were all dead:

2Cr 5:15 And [that] he died for all, that they which live should not henceforth live unto themselves, but unto him which died for them, and rose again.

2Cr 5:16 Wherefore henceforth know we no man after the flesh: yea, though we have known Christ after the flesh, yet now henceforth know we [him] no more.

2Cr 5:17 Therefore if any man [be] in Christ, [he is] a new creature: old things are passed away; behold, all things are become new.

2Cr 5:18 And all things [are] of God, who hath reconciled us to himself by Jesus Christ, and hath given to us the ministry of reconciliation;
2Cr 5:19 To wit, that God was in Christ, reconciling the world unto himself, not imputing their trespasses unto them; and hath committed unto us the word of reconciliation.
2Cr 5:20 Now then we are ambassadors for Christ, as though God did beseech [you] by us: we pray [you] in Christ's stead, be ye reconciled to God.

2Cr 5:21 For he hath made him [to be] sin for us, who knew no sin; that we might be made the righteousness of God in him.
Rom 4:25 Who was delivered for our offences, and was raised again for our justification.

Our existence was not our choice. Our flesh cannot inherit incorruption. Our choices, the exercise of our own will, "WHO WE ARE", is what is given to us. Choice transcends our birth, it is utterly personal. Before us then is either the lust of the flesh or the obedience of the spirit. Our fruit ripens from the seed of our choices. Will our fruit align with God? Again, ask yourself, "What will be my name when God speaks with me?" We freely choose what our outcome will be within our own existence framed by the birth and death of the flesh, now, or at the end of our time on earth. It is our own edenic choice.

2Cr 1:1 Paul, an apostle of Jesus Christ by the will of God
1Jo 2:17 And the world passeth away, and the lust thereof: but he that doeth the will of God abideth for ever.
Act 4:36 And Joses, who by the apostles was surnamed Barnabas, (which is, being interpreted, the son of consolation,)
Rom12:2 And be not conformed to this world: but be ye transformed by the renewing of your mind, that ye

may prove what [is] that good, and acceptable, and perfect, will of God.

1Cr 15:46 Howbeit that [was] not first which is spiritual, but that which is natural; and afterward that which is spiritual.

Rom15:6 That ye may with one mind [and] one mouth glorify God, even the Father of our Lord Jesus Christ.

Col 3:2 Set your affection on things above, not on things on the earth.

Col 3:3 For ye are dead, and your life is hid with Christ in God.

Col 3:4 When Christ, [who is] our life, shall appear, then shall ye also appear with him in glory.

1Pe 5:4 And when the chief Shepherd shall appear, ye shall receive a crown of glory that fadeth not away.

1Pe 5:5 Likewise, ye younger, submit yourselves unto the elder. Yea, all [of you] be subject one to another, and be clothed with humility: for God resisteth the proud, and giveth grace to the humble.

1Pe 5:6 Humble yourselves therefore under the mighty hand of God, that he may exalt you in due time:

1Pe 5:7 Casting all your care upon him; for he careth for you.

1Pe 5:8 Be sober, be vigilant; because your adversary the devil, as a roaring lion, walketh about, seeking whom he may devour:

1Pe 5:9 Whom resist stedfast in the faith, knowing that the same afflictions are accomplished in your brethren that are in the world.

1Pe 5:10 But the God of all grace, who hath called us unto his eternal glory by Christ Jesus, after that ye have suffered a while, make you perfect, stablish, strengthen, settle [you].

1Pe 5:11 To him [be] glory and dominion for ever and ever. Amen.

Rev 12:11 And they overcame him by the blood of the Lamb, and by the word of their testimony; and they loved not their lives unto the death.

Chapter 10

The Kingdom of God on Earth

Luke 17:20 notes that the Pharisees demanded Jesus to tell them when the Kingdom of God should come. Jesus replied that the Kingdom of God comes without observation. This kingdom is not enacted or proclaimed as all human government must be. Creation is the Kingdom of God yet is unknown to those living who do not know their Creator. God is. The Kingdom of God will come to be known by all His creatures now, or at the judgment. Jesus elsewhere rejoiced that God did not reveal things to the wise and prudent but to babes. Pride desires to alter God's truth to sinners' counterfeit creation; it is enmity to God. The rulers of that time and the nation Israel were seeking their kingdom as they conceived it. It is not possible for anyone focused on the physical to perceive the spiritual. After all, our life with God in His Garden of Eden ended as Adam and Eve exercised their preference, not His will. Humanity does not comprehend God, do not perceive His intent. Jesus startles, astounds, and befuddles people with a message that is hard to understand for a race of a different mind.

Gen 15:7 And he said unto him, I [am] the LORD that brought thee out of Ur of the Chaldees, to give thee this land to inherit it.

Exd 3:14 And God said unto Moses, I AM THAT I AM: and he said, Thus shalt thou say unto the children of Israel, I AM hath sent me unto you.

Exd 7:5 And the Egyptians shall know that I [am] the LORD, when I stretch forth mine hand upon Egypt, and bring out the children of Israel from among them.

Exd 10:2 And that thou mayest tell in the ears of thy son, and of thy son's son, what things I have wrought in Egypt, and my signs which I have done among them; that ye may know how that I [am] the LORD.

Isa 51:15 But I [am] the LORD thy God, which divided the sea, whose waves roared: The LORD of hosts [is] his name.

Isa 52:6 Therefore my people shall know my name: therefore [they shall know] in that day that I [am] he that doth speak: behold, [it is] I

Mat 16:15 He saith unto them, But whom say ye that I am?

Mar 4:39 And he arose, and rebuked the wind, and said unto the sea, Peace, be still. And the wind ceased, and there was a great calm.

Mar 8:27 And Jesus went out, and his disciples, into the towns of Caesarea Philippi: and by the way he asked his disciples, saying unto them, Whom do men say that I am?

Mar 8:29 And he saith unto them, But whom say ye that I am? And Peter answereth and saith unto him, Thou art the Christ.

Jhn 18:5 They answered him, Jesus of Nazareth. Jesus saith unto them, I am [he]. And Judas also, which betrayed him, stood with them.

Jhn 18:6 As soon then as he had said unto them, I am [he], they went backward, and fell to the ground.

Act 13:40 Beware therefore, lest that come upon you, which is spoken of in the prophets;

Act 13:41 Behold, ye despisers, and wonder, and perish: for I work a work in your days, a work which ye shall in no wise believe, though a man declare it unto you.

1Cr 1:22 For the Jews require a sign, and the Greeks seek after wisdom

Luk 10:21 In that hour Jesus rejoiced in spirit, and said, I thank thee, O Father, Lord of heaven and earth, that thou hast hid these things from the wise and prudent, and hast revealed them unto babes: even so, Father; for so it seemed good in thy sight.

Luk 17:20 And when he was demanded of the Pharisees, when the kingdom of God should come, he answered them and said, The kingdom of God cometh not with observation:

Luk 17:21 Neither shall they say, Lo here! or, lo there! for, behold, the kingdom of God is within you.

Luk 19:10 For the Son of man is come to seek and to save that which was lost.

Luk 19:11 And as they heard these things, he added and spake a parable, because he was nigh to Jerusalem, and because they thought that the kingdom of God should immediately appear.

Mar 1:14 Now after that John was put in prison, Jesus came into Galilee, preaching the gospel of the kingdom of God,

Mar 1:15 And saying, The time is fulfilled, and the kingdom of God is at hand: repent ye, and believe the gospel.

Mar 10:14 But when Jesus saw [it], he was much displeased, and said unto them, Suffer the little children to come unto me, and forbid them not: for of such is the kingdom of God.

Mar 10:15 Verily I say unto you, Whosoever shall not receive the kingdom of God as a little child, he shall not enter therein.

Mar 12:28 And one of the scribes came, and having heard them reasoning together, and perceiving that he had answered them well, asked him, Which is the first commandment of all?

Mar 12:29 And Jesus answered him, The first of all the commandments [is], Hear, O Israel; The Lord our God is one Lord:

Mar 12:30 And thou shalt love the Lord thy God with all thy heart, and with all thy soul, and with all thy mind, and with all thy strength: this [is] the first commandment.

Mar 12:31 And the second [is] like, [namely] this, Thou shalt love thy neighbour as thyself. There is none other commandment greater than these.

Mar 12:32 And the scribe said unto him, Well, Master, thou hast said the truth: for there is one God; and there is none other but he:

Mar 12:33 And to love him with all the heart, and with all the understanding, and with all the soul, and with all the strength, and to love [his] neighbour as himself, is more than all whole burnt offerings and sacrifices.

Mar 12:34 And when Jesus saw that he answered discreetly, he said unto him, Thou art not far from the kingdom of God. And no man after that durst ask him [any question].

Luk 12:30 For all these things do the nations of the world seek after: and your Father knoweth that ye have need of these things.

Luk 12:31 But rather seek ye the kingdom of God; and all these things shall be added unto you.

Luk 12:32 Fear not, little flock; for it is your Father's good pleasure to give you the kingdom.

Jhn 3:3 Jesus answered and said unto him, Verily, verily, I say unto thee, Except a man be born again, he cannot see the kingdom of God.

Jhn 3:4 Nicodemus saith unto him, How can a man be born when he is old? can he enter the second time into his mother's womb, and be born?

Jhn 3:5 Jesus answered, Verily, verily, I say unto thee, Except a man be born of water and [of] the Spirit, he cannot enter into the kingdom of God.

Jhn 3:6 That which is born of the flesh is flesh; and that which is born of the Spirit is spirit.

Jhn 3:7 Marvel not that I said unto thee, Ye must be born again.

Jhn 3:8 The wind bloweth where it listeth, and thou hearest the sound thereof, but canst not tell whence it

cometh, and whither it goeth: so is every one that is born of the Spirit.
Jhn 3:9 Nicodemus answered and said unto him, How can these things be?
Jhn 3:10 Jesus answered and said unto him, Art thou a master of Israel, and knowest not these things?

"The Kingdom of God is within you." Kingdom is a volatile word in human knowing, all who suffer inadequate governance. Jesus plainly states:

Jhn 18:36 Jesus answered, my kingdom is not of this world: if my kingdom were of this world, then would my servants fight, that I should not be delivered to the Jews: but now is my kingdom not from hence.
Jhn 18:37 Pilate therefore said unto him, Art thou a king then? Jesus answered, Thou sayest that I am a king. To this end was I born, and for this cause came I into the world, that I should bear witness unto the truth. Every one that is of the truth heareth my voice.

Jesus was born to bear witness unto the truth, everyone that is of the truth hears His voice. The Kingdom of God is not of this world. That which is born of flesh is flesh. Jesus insists a person must be born again to see the Kingdom of God. A person must be born of the Spirit because that which is born of the Spirit is spirit. The Kingdom of God is within us. Whoever would must receive the Kingdom of God as a little child. The conditions for the Kingdom of God indicate that it is not entered by reasoning or by any possible physical accomplishment. The Kingdom of God is not coercion, it is chosen by those who accept the gospel, the testimony of Jesus.

Psa 40:8 I delight to do thy will, O my God: yea, thy law [is] within my heart.

Mat 5:10 Blessed [are] they which are persecuted for righteousness' sake: for theirs is the kingdom of heaven.
Luk 11:28 But he said, Yea rather, blessed [are] they that hear the word of God, and keep it.
Jhn 20:29 Jesus saith unto him, Thomas, because thou hast seen me, thou hast believed: blessed [are] they that have not seen, and [yet] have believed.
Rev 2:7 He that hath an ear, let him hear what the Spirit saith unto the churches; To him that overcometh will I give to eat of the tree of life, which is in the midst of the paradise of God.
Rev 22:14 Blessed [are] they that do his commandments, that they may have right to the tree of life, and may enter in through the gates into the city.
Rom 6:4 Therefore we are buried with him by baptism into death: that like as Christ was raised up from the dead by the glory of the Father, even so we also should walk in newness of life.
Rom 8:10 And if Christ [be] in you, the body [is] dead because of sin; but the Spirit [is] life because of righteousness.
Rom 8:11 But if the Spirit of him that raised up Jesus from the dead dwell in you, he that raised up Christ from the dead shall also quicken your mortal bodies by his Spirit that dwelleth in you.
Rom 14:17 For the kingdom of God is not meat and drink; but righteousness, and peace, and joy in the Holy Ghost.
Eph 2:1 And you [hath he quickened], who were dead in trespasses and sins;
Eph 2:2 Wherein in time past ye walked according to the course of this world, according to the prince of the power of the air, the spirit that now worketh in the children of disobedience:

Eph 2:3 Among whom also we all had our conversation in times past in the lusts of our flesh, fulfilling the desires of the flesh and of the mind; and were by nature the children of wrath, even as others.
Eph 2:4 But God, who is rich in mercy, for his great love wherewith he loved us,
Eph 2:5 Even when we were dead in sins, hath quickened us together with Christ, (by grace ye are saved;)
Eph 2:6 And hath raised [us] up together, and made [us] sit together in heavenly [places] in Christ Jesus:
Eph 2:7 That in the ages to come he might shew the exceeding riches of his grace in [his] kindness toward us through Christ Jesus.
Eph 2:8 For by grace are ye saved through faith; and that not of yourselves: [it is] the gift of God:
Eph 2:9 Not of works, lest any man should boast.
Eph 2:10 For we are his workmanship, created in Christ Jesus unto good works, which God hath before ordained that we should walk in them.
Rom 4:3 For what saith the scripture? Abraham believed God, and it was counted unto him for righteousness.
Rom 4:4 Now to him that worketh is the reward not reckoned of grace, but of debt.
Rom 4:5 But to him that worketh not, but believeth on him that justifieth the ungodly, his faith is counted for righteousness.
Rom 4:6 Even as David also describeth the blessedness of the man, unto whom God imputeth righteousness without works,
Rom 4:7 [Saying], Blessed [are] they whose iniquities are forgiven, and whose sins are covered.
Rom 4:8 Blessed [is] the man to whom the Lord will not impute sin.

2Cr 1:10 Who delivered us from so great a death, and doth deliver: in whom we trust that he will yet deliver [us];

Gal 1:4 Who gave himself for our sins, that he might deliver us from this present evil world, according to the will of God and our Father:

2Cr 5:18 And all things [are] of God, who hath reconciled us to himself by Jesus Christ, and hath given to us the ministry of reconciliation;

2Cr 5:19 To wit, that God was in Christ, reconciling the world unto himself, not imputing their trespasses unto them; and hath committed unto us the word of reconciliation.

2Cr 5:20 Now then we are ambassadors for Christ, as though God did beseech [you] by us: we pray [you] in Christ's stead, be ye reconciled to God.

2Cr 5:21 For he hath made him [to be] sin for us, who knew no sin; that we might be made the righteousness of God in him.

1Th 4:16 For the Lord himself shall descend from heaven with a shout, with the voice of the archangel, and with the trump of God: and the dead in Christ shall rise first:

Rev 1:5 And from Jesus Christ, [who is] the faithful witness, [and] the first begotten of the dead, and the prince of the kings of the earth. Unto him that loved us, and washed us from our sins in his own blood,

Rev 1:6 And hath made us kings and priests unto God and his Father; to him [be] glory and dominion forever and ever. Amen.

Rev 1:7 Behold, he cometh with clouds; and every eye shall see him, and they [also] which pierced him: and all kindreds of the earth shall wail because of him. Even so, Amen.

Rev 1:8 I am Alpha and Omega, the beginning and the ending, saith the Lord, which is, and which was, and which is to come, the Almighty.

Know the Purpose of God

The Holy Spirit prepares His kingdom as revealed by these ninety-six verses in the order that they occur in the New Testament.

Mat 1:20 But while he thought on these things, behold, the angel of the Lord appeared unto him in a dream, saying, Joseph, thou son of David, fear not to take unto thee Mary thy wife: for that which is conceived in her is of the Holy Ghost.
Mat 3:11 I indeed baptize you with water unto repentance: but he that cometh after me is mightier than I, whose shoes I am not worthy to bear: he shall baptize you with the Holy Ghost, and [with] fire:
Mat 3:16 And Jesus, when he was baptized, went up straightway out of the water: and, lo, the heavens were opened unto him, and he saw the Spirit of God descending like a dove, and lighting upon him:
Mat 4:1 Then was Jesus led up of the Spirit into the wilderness to be tempted of the devil.
Mar 12:36 For David himself said by the Holy Ghost, The LORD said to my Lord, Sit thou on my right hand, till I make thine enemies thy footstool.
Mar 13:11 But when they shall lead [you], and deliver you up, take no thought beforehand what ye shall speak, neither do ye premeditate: but whatsoever shall be given you in that hour, that speak ye: for it is not ye that speak, but the Holy Ghost.
Luk 4:1 And Jesus being full of the Holy Ghost returned from Jordan, and was led by the Spirit into the wilderness,

Luk 4:14 And Jesus returned in the power of the Spirit into Galilee: and there went out a fame of him through all the region round about.

Luk 4:18 The Spirit of the Lord [is] upon me, because He hath anointed me to preach the gospel to the poor; He hath sent me to heal the brokenhearted, to preach deliverance to the captives, and recovering of sight to the blind, to set at liberty them that are bruised,

Jhn 1:32 And John bare record, saying, I saw the Spirit descending from heaven like a dove, and it abode upon him.

Jhn 1:33 And I knew him not: but he that sent me to baptize with water, the same said unto me, Upon whom thou shalt see the Spirit descending, and remaining on him, the same is he which baptizeth with the Holy Ghost.

Jhn 7:39 (But this spake he of the Spirit, which they that believe on him should receive: for the Holy Ghost was not yet [given]; because that Jesus was not yet glorified.)

Jhn 14:18 I will not leave you comfortless: I will come to you.

Jhn 14:26 But the Comforter, [which is] the Holy Ghost, whom the Father will send in my name, he shall teach you all things, and bring all things to your remembrance, whatsoever I have said unto you.

Jhn 20:22 And when he had said this, he breathed on [them], and saith unto them, Receive ye the Holy Ghost:

Act 1:2 Until the day in which he was taken up, after that he through the Holy Ghost had given commandments unto the apostles whom he had chosen:

Act 1:5 For John truly baptized with water; but ye shall be baptized with the Holy Ghost not many days hence.

Act 1:8 But ye shall receive power, after that the Holy Ghost is come upon you: and ye shall be witnesses unto me both in Jerusalem, and in all Judaea, and in Samaria, and unto the uttermost part of the earth.

Act 2:4 And they were all filled with the Holy Ghost, and began to speak with other tongues, as the Spirit gave them utterance.

Act 2:33 Therefore being by the right hand of God exalted, and having received of the Father the promise of the Holy Ghost, he hath shed forth this, which ye now see and hear.

Act 2:38 Then Peter said unto them, Repent, and be baptized every one of you in the name of Jesus Christ for the remission of sins, and ye shall receive the gift of the Holy Ghost.

Act 2:39 For the promise is unto you, and to your children, and to all that are afar off, [even] as many as the Lord our God shall call.

Act 4:8 Then Peter, filled with the Holy Ghost, said unto them, Ye rulers of the people, and elders of Israel,

Act 4:31 And when they had prayed, the place was shaken where they were assembled together; and they were all filled with the Holy Ghost, and they spake the word of God with boldness.

Act 5:32 And we are his witnesses of these things; and [so is] also the Holy Ghost, whom God hath given to them that obey him.

Act 6:3 Wherefore, brethren, look ye out among you seven men of honest report, full of the Holy Ghost and wisdom, whom we may appoint over this business.

Act 6:5 And the saying pleased the whole multitude: and they chose Stephen, a man full of faith and of the Holy Ghost, and Philip, and Prochorus, and Nicanor, and Timon, and Parmenas, and Nicolas a proselyte of Antioch:

Act 7:51 Ye stiffnecked and uncircumcised in heart and ears, ye do always resist the Holy Ghost: as your fathers [did], so [do] ye.

Act 7:55 But he, being full of the Holy Ghost, looked up stedfastly into heaven, and saw the glory of God, and Jesus standing on the right hand of God,

Act 8:15 who, when they were come down, prayed for them, that they might receive the Holy Ghost:

Act 8:17 Then laid they [their] hands on them, and they received the Holy Ghost.

Act 8:18 And when Simon saw that through laying on of the apostles' hands the Holy Ghost was given, he offered them money,

Act 8:19 Saying, Give me also this power, that on whomsoever I lay hands, he may receive the Holy Ghost.

Act 8:29 Then the Spirit said unto Philip, Go near, and join thyself to this chariot.

Act 8:39 And when they were come up out of the water, the Spirit of the Lord caught away Philip, that the eunuch saw him no more: and he went on his way rejoicing.

Act 9:17 And Ananias went his way, and entered into the house; and putting his hands on him said, Brother Saul, the Lord, [even] Jesus, that appeared unto thee in the way as thou camest, hath sent me, that thou mightest receive thy sight, and be filled with the Holy Ghost.

Act 9:31 Then had the churches rest throughout all Judaea and Galilee and Samaria, and were edified; and walking in the fear of the Lord, and in the comfort of the Holy Ghost, were multiplied.

Act 10:19 While Peter thought on the vision, the Spirit said unto him, Behold, three men seek thee.

Act 10:38 How God anointed Jesus of Nazareth with the Holy Ghost and with power: who went about doing good, and healing all that were oppressed of the devil; for God was with him.

Act 10:44 While Peter yet spake these words, the Holy Ghost fell on all them which heard the word.

Act 10:45 And they of the circumcision which believed were astonished, as many as came with Peter, because that on the Gentiles also was poured out the gift of the Holy Ghost.

Act 10:47 Can any man forbid water, that these should not be baptized, which have received the Holy Ghost as well as we?

Act 11:12 And the Spirit bade me go with them, nothing doubting. Moreover these six brethren accompanied me, and we entered into the man's house:

Act 11:15 And as I began to speak, the Holy Ghost fell on them, as on us at the beginning.

Act 11:16 Then remembered I the word of the Lord, how that he said, John indeed baptized with water; but ye shall be baptized with the Holy Ghost.

Act 11:24 For he was a good man, and full of the Holy Ghost and of faith: and much people was added unto the Lord.

Act 11:28 And there stood up one of them named Agabus, and signified by the Spirit that there should be great dearth throughout all the world: which came to pass in the days of Claudius Caesar.

Act 13:2 As they ministered to the Lord, and fasted, the Holy Ghost said, Separate me Barnabas and Saul for the work whereunto I have called them.

Act 13:4 So they, being sent forth by the Holy Ghost, departed unto Seleucia; and from thence they sailed to Cyprus.

Act 13:9 Then Saul, (who also [is called] Paul,) filled with the Holy Ghost, set his eyes on him,

Act 13:52 And the disciples were filled with joy, and with the Holy Ghost.

Act 15:8 And God, which knoweth the hearts, bare them witness, giving them the Holy Ghost, even as [he did] unto us;

Act 15:28 For it seemed good to the Holy Ghost, and to us, to lay upon you no greater burden than these necessary things;

Act 16:6 Now when they had gone throughout Phrygia and the region of Galatia, and were forbidden of the Holy Ghost to preach the word in Asia,

Act 16:7 After they were come to Mysia, they assayed to go into Bithynia: but the Spirit suffered them not.

Act 18:5 And when Silas and Timotheus were come from Macedonia, Paul was pressed in the spirit, and testified to the Jews [that] Jesus [was] Christ.

Act 19:2 He said unto them, Have ye received the Holy Ghost since ye believed? And they said unto him, We have not so much as heard whether there be any Holy Ghost.

Act 19:6 And when Paul had laid [his] hands upon them, the Holy Ghost came on them; and they spake with tongues, and prophesied.

Act 20:23 Save that the Holy Ghost witnesseth in every city, saying that bonds and afflictions abide me.

Act 20:28 Take heed therefore unto yourselves, and to all the flock, over the which the Holy Ghost hath made you overseers, to feed the church of God, which he hath purchased with his own blood.

Act 21:11 And when he was come unto us, he took Paul's girdle, and bound his own hands and feet, and said, Thus saith the Holy Ghost, So shall the Jews at Jerusalem bind the man that owneth this girdle, and shall deliver [him] into the hands of the Gentiles.

Act 28:25 And when they agreed not among themselves, they departed, after that Paul had spoken one word, Well spake the Holy Ghost by Esaias the prophet unto our fathers,

Rom 8:14 For as many as are led by the Spirit of God, they are the sons of God.

Rom 8:16 The Spirit itself beareth witness with our spirit, that we are the children of God:

Rom 8:23 And not only [they], but ourselves also, which have the firstfruits of the Spirit, even we ourselves groan within ourselves, waiting for the adoption, [to wit], the redemption of our body.

Rom 8:26 Likewise the Spirit also helpeth our infirmities: for we know not what we should pray for as we ought: but the Spirit itself maketh intercession for us with groanings which cannot be uttered.

Rom 8:27 And He that searcheth the hearts knoweth what [is] the mind of the Spirit, because He maketh intercession for the saints according to [the will of] God.

Rom 9:1 I say the truth in Christ, I lie not, my conscience also bearing me witness in the Holy Ghost,

Rom 14:17 For the kingdom of God is not meat and drink; but righteousness, and peace, and joy in the Holy Ghost.

Rom 15:13 Now the God of hope fill you with all joy and peace in believing, that ye may abound in hope, through the power of the Holy Ghost.

Rom 15:16 That I should be the minister of Jesus Christ to the Gentiles, ministering the gospel of God, that the offering up of the Gentiles might be acceptable, being sanctified by the Holy Ghost.

Rom 15:19 Through mighty signs and wonders, by the power of the Spirit of God; so that from Jerusalem, and round about unto Illyricum, I have fully preached the gospel of Christ.

Rom 15:30 Now I beseech you, brethren, for the Lord Jesus Christ's sake, and for the love of the Spirit, that ye strive together with me in [your] prayers to God for me;

1Cr 2:4 And my speech and my preaching [was] not with enticing words of man's wisdom, but in demonstration of the Spirit and of power:

1Cr 2:10 But God hath revealed [them] unto us by His Spirit: for the Spirit searcheth all things, yea, the deep things of God.

1Cr 2:11 For what man knoweth the things of a man, save the spirit of man which is in him? even so the things of God knoweth no man, but the Spirit of God.

1Cr 2:12 Now we have received, not the spirit of the world, but the Spirit which is of God; that we might know the things that are freely given to us of God.

1Cr 2:13 Which things also we speak, not in the words which man's wisdom teacheth, but which the Holy Ghost teacheth; comparing spiritual things with spiritual.

1Cr 2:14 But the natural man receiveth not the things of the Spirit of God: for they are foolishness unto him: neither can he know [them], because they are spiritually discerned.

1Cr 3:16 Know ye not that ye are the temple of God, and [that] the Spirit of God dwelleth in you?

1Cr 6:11 And such were some of you: but ye are washed, but ye are sanctified, but ye are justified in the name of the Lord Jesus, and by the Spirit of our God.

1Cr 6:17 But he that is joined unto the Lord is one spirit.

1Cr 6:19 What? know ye not that your body is the temple of the Holy Ghost [which is] in you, which ye have of God, and ye are not your own?

1Cr 6:20 For ye are bought with a price: therefore glorify God in your body, and in your spirit, which are God's.

Gal 5:18 But if ye be led of the Spirit, ye are not under the law.

Gal 5:22 But the fruit of the Spirit is love, joy, peace, longsuffering, gentleness, goodness, faith,
Gal 5:23 Meekness, temperance: against such there is no law.
Gal 5:24 And they that are Christ's have crucified the flesh with the affections and lusts.
Gal 5:25 If we live in the Spirit, let us also walk in the Spirit.
Eph 1:13 In whom ye also [trusted], after that ye heard the word of truth, the gospel of your salvation: in whom also after that ye believed, ye were sealed with that holy Spirit of promise,
Rev 2:29 He that hath an ear, let him hear what the Spirit saith unto the churches.
Rev 3:6 He that hath an ear, let him hear what the Spirit saith unto the churches.
Rev 3:13 He that hath an ear, let him hear what the Spirit saith unto the churches.
Rev 3:22 He that hath an ear, let him hear what the Spirit saith unto the churches.
Rev 22:6 And he said unto me, These sayings [are] faithful and true: and the Lord God of the holy prophets sent His angel to shew unto his servants the things which must shortly be done.
Rev 22:16 I Jesus have sent mine angel to testify unto you these things in the churches. I am the root and the offspring of David, [and] the bright and morning star.

Chapter 11

Jesus the Son of Man

The creator and the last Adam is the Lord, God. The last Adam because He is the glory of God and human being that God created and knew even before the fall and throughout the ages of human being onto the completion of the human creation experience. The appellation, "the last Adam", recognizes the end to the entirety of human creation. Human being fulfills the Word of God by existing in God who God has created to His glory. The end arrives at fulfillment of the beginning. Humans who are the image and likeness of God fulfill the purpose of His expectation.

Gen 1:26 And God said, Let us make man in our image, after our likeness: and let them have dominion over the fish of the sea, and over the fowl of the air, and over the cattle, and over all the earth, and over every creeping thing that creepeth upon the earth
Gen 5:1 This [is] the book of the generations of Adam. In the day that God created man, in the likeness of God made He him;
Gen 5:2 Male and female created He them; and blessed them, and called their name Adam, in the day when they were created.
Jhn 17:5 And now, O Father, glorify thou me with thine own self with the glory which I had with thee before the world was.
1Cr 2:7 But we speak the wisdom of God in a mystery, [even] the hidden [wisdom], which God ordained before the world unto our glory:
2Ti 1:9 Who hath saved us, and called [us] with an holy calling, not according to our works, but according to his own purpose and grace, which was given us in Christ Jesus before the world began,
Tts 1:2 In hope of eternal life, which God, that cannot lie, promised before the world began;

Gal 4:4 But when the fulness of the time was come, God sent forth his Son, made of a woman, made under the law,

2Cr 5:21 For he hath made him [to be] sin for us, who knew no sin; that we might be made the righteousness of God in him.

1Cr 15:45 And so it is written, The first man Adam was made a living soul; the last Adam [was made] a quickening spirit.

1Cr 15:47 The first man [is] of the earth, earthy: the second man [is] the Lord from heaven.

Rev 1:8 I am Alpha and Omega, the beginning and the ending, saith the Lord, which is, and which was, and which is to come, the Almighty.

Rev 21:6 And he said unto me, It is done. I am Alpha and Omega, the beginning and the end. I will give unto him that is athirst of the fountain of the water of life freely.

Rev 22:13 I am Alpha and Omega, the beginning and the end, the first and the last.

Luk 12:32 Fear not, little flock; for it is your Father's good pleasure to give you the kingdom.

The End of Time

It is the Spirit of God that was rent from Adam and Eve. The Holy Spirit is returned to willing humans, the promise, God in us is true treasure and wholly unattainable otherwise. God is the true creator Who is unlimited by the impossible and so He also is the Recreator. The Holy Spirit impregnated the virgin, was born in the flesh, Who is the Word of God fulfilled. Fulfilled expresses attainment or satisfaction of a purpose. The function of time then is drawing to conclusion. Death will die. Without death there is no need for time. The mystery of God will then be finished.

Rev 10:6 And sware by him that liveth for ever and ever, who created heaven, and the things that therein are, and the earth, and the things that therein are, and the sea, and the things which are therein, that there should be time no longer:

Rev 10:7 but in the days of the voice of the seventh angel, when he shall begin to sound, the mystery of God should be finished, as he hath declared to his servants the prophets.

Rev 19:10 And I fell at his feet to worship him. And he said unto me, See [thou do it] not: I am thy fellowservant, and of thy brethren that have the testimony of Jesus: worship God: for the testimony of Jesus is the spirit of prophecy.

Eph 1:17 That the God of our Lord Jesus Christ, the Father of glory, may give unto you the spirit of wisdom and revelation in the knowledge of him:

Eph 1:18 The eyes of your understanding being enlightened; that ye may know what is the hope of his calling, and what the riches of the glory of his inheritance in the saints,

Eph 1:19 And what [is] the exceeding greatness of his power to us-ward who believe, according to the working of his mighty power,

Eph 1:20 Which he wrought in Christ, when he raised him from the dead, and set [him] at his own right hand in the heavenly [places],

Eph 1:21 Far above all principality, and power, and might, and dominion, and every name that is named, not only in this world, but also in that which is to come:

Eph 1:22 And hath put all [things] under his feet, and gave him [to be] the head over all [things] to the church,

Eph 1:23 Which is his body, the fulness of him that filleth all in all.

1Cr 15:28 And when all things shall be subdued unto him, then shall the Son also himself be subject unto him that put all things under him, that God may be all in all.

Col 1:27 To whom God would make known what [is] the riches of the glory of this mystery among the Gentiles; which is Christ in you, the hope of glory:

1Ti 3:16 And without controversy great is the mystery of godliness: God was manifest in the flesh, justified in the Spirit, seen of angels, preached unto the Gentiles, believed on in the world, received up into glory.

Mat 9:12 But when Jesus heard [that], he said unto them, They that be whole need not a physician, but they that are sick.

Mat 9:13 But go ye and learn what [that] meaneth, I will have mercy, and not sacrifice: for I am not come to call the righteous, but sinners to repentance.

Jhn 12:26 If any man serve me, let him follow me; and where I am, there shall also my servant be: if any man serve me, him will [my] Father honour.

Jhn 12:27 Now is my soul troubled; and what shall I say? Father, save me from this hour: but for this cause came I unto this hour.

Jhn 12:28 Father, glorify thy name. Then came there a voice from heaven, [saying], I have both glorified [it], and will glorify [it] again.

Jhn 12:29 The people therefore, that stood by, and heard [it], said that it thundered: others said, An angel spake to him.

Jhn 12:30 Jesus answered and said, This voice came not because of me, but for your sakes.

Jhn 12:31Now is the judgment of this world: now shall the prince of this world be cast out.

Jhn 12:32 And I, if I be lifted up from the earth, will draw all [men] unto me.

Jhn 12:33 This he said, signifying what death he should die.

Jhn 12:34 The people answered him, We have heard out of the law that Christ abideth for ever: and how sayest thou, The Son of man must be lifted up? who is this Son of man?

Jhn 12:35 Then Jesus said unto them, Yet a little while is the light with you. Walk while ye have the light, lest darkness come upon you: for he that walketh in darkness knoweth not whither he goeth.

Jhn 12:36 While ye have light, believe in the light, that ye may be the children of light. These things spake Jesus, and departed, and did hide himself from them.

Jhn 12:37 But though he had done so many miracles before them, yet they believed not on him:

Jhn 12:38 That the saying of Esaias the prophet might be fulfilled, which he spake, Lord, who hath believed our report? and to whom hath the arm of the Lord been revealed?

Jhn 12:39 Therefore they could not believe, because that Esaias said again,

Jhn 12:40 He hath blinded their eyes, and hardened their heart; that they should not see with [their] eyes, nor understand with [their] heart, and be converted, and I should heal them.

Jhn 12:41These things said Esaias, when he saw his glory, and spake of him.

Jhn 12:42 Nevertheless among the chief rulers also many believed on him; but because of the Pharisees they did not confess [him], lest they should be put out of the synagogue:

Jhn 12:43 For they loved the praise of men more than the praise of God.

Jhn 12:44 Jesus cried and said, He that believeth on me, believeth not on me, but on him that sent me.

Jhn 12:45 And he that seeth me seeth him that sent me.

Jhn 12:46 I am come a light into the world, that whosoever believeth on me should not abide in darkness.
Jhn 12:47 And if any man hear my words, and believe not, I judge him not: for I came not to judge the world, but to save the world.
Jhn 12:48 He that rejecteth me, and receiveth not my words, hath one that judgeth him: the word that I have spoken, the same shall judge him in the last day.
Jhn 12:49 For I have not spoken of myself; but the Father which sent me, he gave me a commandment, what I should say, and what I should speak.
Jhn 12:50 And I know that his commandment is life everlasting: whatsoever I speak therefore, even as the Father said unto me, so I speak.

Jhn 1:12 But as many as received him, to them gave he power to become the sons of God, [even] to them that believe on his name:
Jhn 1:13 Which were born, not of blood, nor of the will of the flesh, nor of the will of man, but of God.
Eph 4:6 One God and Father of all, who [is] above all, and through all, and in you all.
Eph 4:7 But unto every one of us is given grace according to the measure of the gift of Christ.
Eph 4:8 Wherefore He saith, When He ascended up on high, He led captivity captive, and gave gifts unto men.
Eph 4:11 And He gave some, apostles; and some, prophets; and some, evangelists; and some, pastors and teachers;
Eph 4:12 For the perfecting of the saints, for the work of the ministry, for the edifying of the body of Christ:
Eph 4:13 Till we all come in the unity of the faith, and of the knowledge of the Son of God, unto a perfect man, unto the measure of the stature of the fulness of Christ:

Eph 4:14 That we [henceforth] be no more children, tossed to and fro, and carried about with every wind of doctrine, by the sleight of men, [and] cunning craftiness, whereby they lie in wait to deceive;
Eph 4:15 But speaking the truth in love, may grow up into him in all things, which is the head, [even] Christ:
Eph 4:16 From whom the whole body fitly joined together and compacted by that which every joint supplieth, according to the effectual working in the measure of every part, maketh increase of the body unto the edifying of itself in love.
Eph 1:23 Which is his body, the fulness of him that filleth all in all.

Hbr 10:20 By a new and living way, which he hath consecrated for us, through the veil, that is to say, his flesh;
Hbr 10:21 And [having] an high priest over the house of God;
Hbr 10:22 Let us draw near with a true heart in full assurance of faith, having our hearts sprinkled from an evil conscience, and our bodies washed with pure water.
Hbr 10:23 Let us hold fast the profession of [our] faith without wavering; (for he [is] faithful that promised;)
Hbr 10:24 And let us consider one another to provoke unto love and to good works:
Hbr 10:25 Not forsaking the assembling of ourselves together, as the manner of some [is]; but exhorting [one another]: and so much the more, as ye see the day approaching.

Act 1:2 Until the day in which he was taken up, after that He through the Holy Ghost had given commandments unto the apostles whom He had chosen:

Act 1:3 To whom also He shewed himself alive after His passion by many infallible proofs, being seen of them forty days, and speaking of the things pertaining to the kingdom of God:

Act 1:4 And, being assembled together with [them], commanded them that they should not depart from Jerusalem, but wait for the promise of the Father, which, [saith He], ye have heard of Me.

Act 1:5 For John truly baptized with water; but ye shall be baptized with the Holy Ghost not many days hence.

Act 1:6 When they therefore were come together, they asked of him, saying, Lord, wilt thou at this time restore again the kingdom to Israel?

Act 1:7 And He said unto them, It is not for you to know the times or the seasons, which the Father hath put in His own power.

Act 1:8 But ye shall receive power, after that the Holy Ghost is come upon you: and ye shall be witnesses unto Me both in Jerusalem, and in all Judaea, and in Samaria, and unto the uttermost part of the earth.

2Cr 11:3 But I fear, lest by any means, as the serpent beguiled Eve through his subtilty, so your minds should be corrupted from the simplicity that is in Christ.

Psa 103:4 Who redeemeth thy life from destruction; Who crowneth thee with lovingkindness and tender mercies;

Psa 69:16 Hear me, O LORD; for thy lovingkindness [is] good: turn unto me according to the multitude of thy tender mercies.

Psa 40:10 I have not hid thy righteousness within my heart; I have declared thy faithfulness and thy salvation: I have not concealed thy lovingkindness and thy truth from the great congregation.

Act 20:28 Take heed therefore unto yourselves, and to all the flock, over the which the Holy Ghost hath made you overseers, to feed the church of God, which he hath purchased with his own blood.

Rom 1:7 To all that be in Rome, beloved of God, called [to be] saints: Grace to you and peace from God our Father, and the Lord Jesus Christ.

1Cr 1:2 Unto the church of God which is at Corinth, to them that are sanctified in Christ Jesus, called [to be] saints, with all that in every place call upon the name of Jesus Christ our Lord, both theirs and ours:

1Th 1:1 Paul, and Silvanus, and Timotheus, unto the church of the Thessalonians [which is] in God the Father and [in] the Lord Jesus Christ: Grace [be] unto you, and peace, from God our Father, and the Lord Jesus Christ.

Hbr 12:23 To the general assembly and church of the firstborn, which are written in heaven, and to God the Judge of all, and to the spirits of just men made perfect,

Col 1:18 And He is the head of the body, the church: who is the beginning, the firstborn from the dead; that in all [things] He might have the preeminence.

Eph 1:18 The eyes of your understanding being enlightened; that ye may know what is the hope of His calling, and what the riches of the glory of His inheritance in the saints,

Eph 1:22 And hath put all [things] under His feet, and gave Him [to be] the head over all [things] to the church,

Eph 3:10 To the intent that now unto the principalities and powers in heavenly [places] might be known by the church the manifold wisdom of God,

Act 2:39 For the promise is unto you, and to your children, and to all that are afar off, [even] as many as the Lord our God shall call.

Eph 2:19 Now therefore ye are no more strangers and foreigners, but fellowcitizens with the saints, and of the household of God;
Col 3:10 And have put on the new [man], which is renewed in knowledge after the image of him that created him:

Jesus is the Son of Man, the sacrifice, propitiation, the last Adam to redeem all His brethren who are otherwise dead, hopelessly lost to destruction. Jesus spent his lifeblood to create His children, full of the Spirit of God of anyone who will accept Him. Humans as God initially purposed and yet now different, burned, tempered, proven through the flames of choice, who are, not by humanity's common birth but choosing to be and willfully spiritual by the grace of God to the praise of His supreme Glory. God spoke, He healed, He visited His expectation and gifts to bring about His will on Earth as it is in Heaven; God in the flesh to accomplish, to deliver His will personally. The Son of Man committed His message for all children of man. Who may become God's own children, who choose the family of God, who then truly are the children of God. Those who choose to be children in the image of their father Who is the God Who chooses to create.

2Cr 5:18 and all things [are] of God, who hath reconciled us to Himself by Jesus Christ, and hath given to us the ministry of reconciliation;
2Cr 5:19 To wit, that God was in Christ, reconciling the world unto Himself, not imputing their trespasses unto them; and hath committed unto us the word of reconciliation.
2Cr 5:20 Now then we are ambassadors for Christ, as though God did beseech [you] by us: we pray [you] in Christ's stead, be ye reconciled to God.
2Cr 5:21 For he hath made him [to be] sin for us, who knew no sin; that we might be made the righteousness of God in him.

Mat 12:8 For the Son of man is Lord even of the sabbath day.

Mat 13:37 He answered and said unto them, He that soweth the good seed is the Son of man;

Mat 18:11 For the Son of man is come to save that which was lost.

Mat 20:28 Even as the Son of man came not to be ministered unto, but to minister, and to give his life a ransom for many.

Luk 4:18 The Spirit of the Lord [is] upon me, because he hath anointed me to preach the gospel to the poor; he hath sent me to heal the brokenhearted, to preach deliverance to the captives, and recovering of sight to the blind, to set at liberty them that are bruised,

Luk 4:19 To preach the acceptable year of the Lord.

Luk 5:24 But that ye may know that the Son of man hath power upon earth to forgive sins, (he said unto the sick of the palsy,) I say unto thee, Arise, and take up thy couch, and go into thine house.

Luk 6:5 And he said unto them, That the Son of man is Lord also of the sabbath.

Luk 9:58 And Jesus said unto him, Foxes have holes, and birds of the air [have] nests; but the Son of man hath not where to lay [his] head.

Luk 19:10 For the Son of man is come to seek and to save that which was lost.

Mat 9:6 But that ye may know that the Son of man hath power on earth to forgive sins, (then saith he to the sick of the palsy,) Arise, take up thy bed, and go unto thine house.

Mat 11:27 All things are delivered unto me of my Father: and no man knoweth the Son, but the Father; neither knoweth any man the Father, save the Son, and [he] to whomsoever the Son will reveal [him].

Jhn 8:28 Then said Jesus unto them, When ye have lifted up the Son of man, then shall ye know that I am

[He], and [that] I do nothing of myself; but as my Father hath taught me, I speak these things.

Jhn 14:9 Jesus saith unto him, Have I been so long time with you, and yet hast thou not known me, Philip? he that hath seen me hath seen the Father; and how sayest thou [then], Shew us the Father?

Jhn 14:12 Verily, verily, I say unto you, He that believeth on me, the works that I do shall he do also; and greater [works] than these shall he do; because I go unto my Father.

Jhn 14:16 And I will pray the Father, and he shall give you another Comforter, that he may abide with you for ever;

Jhn 14:17[Even] the Spirit of truth; whom the world cannot receive, because it seeth him not, neither knoweth him: but ye know him; for he dwelleth with you, and shall be in you.

Jhn 14:18 I will not leave you comfortless: I will come to you.

Jhn 14:19 Yet a little while, and the world seeth me no more; but ye see me: because I live, ye shall live also.

Jhn 14:20 At that day ye shall know that I [am] in my Father, and ye in me, and I in you.

1Pe 1:7 That the trial of your faith, being much more precious than of gold that perisheth, though it be tried with fire, might be found unto praise and honour and glory at the appearing of Jesus Christ:

1Pe 1:8 Whom having not seen, ye love; in whom, though now ye see [him] not, yet believing, ye rejoice with joy unspeakable and full of glory:

1Pe 1:9 Receiving the end of your faith, [even] the salvation of [your] souls.

1Pe 1:10 Of which salvation the prophets have enquired and searched diligently, who prophesied of the grace [that should come] unto you:

1Pe 1:11 Searching what, or what manner of time the Spirit of Christ which was in them did signify, when it testified beforehand the sufferings of Christ, and the glory that should follow.

1Pe 1:12 Unto whom it was revealed, that not unto themselves, but unto us they did minister the things, which are now reported unto you by them that have preached the gospel unto you with the Holy Ghost sent down from heaven; which things the angels desire to look into.

1Pe 1:13 Wherefore gird up the loins of your mind, be sober, and hope to the end for the grace that is to be brought unto you at the revelation of Jesus Christ

Eph 5:2 And walk in love, as Christ also hath loved us, and hath given himself for us an offering and a sacrifice to God for a sweetsmelling savour.

Hbr 7:27 Who needeth not daily, as those high priests, to offer up sacrifice, first for his own sins, and then for the people's: for this he did once, when he offered up himself.

Hbr 9:26 For then must he often have suffered since the foundation of the world: but now once in the end of the world hath he appeared to put away sin by the sacrifice of himself.

Rom 3:25 Whom God hath set forth [to be] a propitiation through faith in his blood, to declare his righteousness for the remission of sins that are past, through the forbearance of God;

Rom 3:26 To declare, [I say], at this time his righteousness: that he might be just, and the justifier of him which believeth in Jesus.

1Pe 1:7 That the trial of your faith, being much more precious than of gold that perisheth, though it be tried with fire, might be found unto praise and honour and glory at the appearing of Jesus Christ:

Rev 3:18 I counsel thee to buy of me gold tried in the fire, that thou mayest be rich; and white raiment, that thou mayest be clothed, and [that] the shame of thy nakedness do not appear; and anoint thine eyes with eyesalve, that thou mayest see.

2Cr 6:16 And what agreement hath the temple of God with idols? for ye are the temple of the living God; as God hath said, I will dwell in them, and walk in [them]; and I will be their God, and they shall be my people.

2Cr 6:17 Wherefore come out from among them, and be ye separate, saith the Lord, and touch not the unclean [thing]; and I will receive you,

2Cr 6:18 And will be a Father unto you, and ye shall be my sons and daughters, saith the Lord Almighty.

Luk 20:35 But they which shall be accounted worthy to obtain that world, and the resurrection from the dead, neither marry, nor are given in marriage:

Luk 20:36 Neither can they die any more: for they are equal unto the angels; and are the children of God, being the children of the resurrection.

Psa 8:4 What is man, that thou art mindful of him? and the son of man, that thou visitest him?

Psa 8:5 For thou hast made him a little lower than the angels, and hast crowned him with glory and honour.

Jesus was entirely focused on God's will.

Mat 3:17 And lo a voice from heaven, saying, This is my beloved Son, in whom I am well pleased.

Mat 12:18 Behold my servant, whom I have chosen; my beloved, in whom my soul is well pleased: I will put my spirit upon him, and he shall shew judgment to the Gentiles.

Mat 17:5 While he yet spake, behold, a bright cloud overshadowed them: and behold a voice out of the cloud, which said, This is my beloved Son, in whom I am well pleased; hear ye him.

Mar 1:11 And there came a voice from heaven, [saying], Thou art my beloved Son, in whom I am well pleased.

Luk 3:22 And the Holy Ghost descended in a bodily shape like a dove upon him, and a voice came from heaven, which said, Thou art my beloved Son; in thee I am well pleased.

Psa 8:4 What is man, that thou art mindful of him? and the son of man, that thou visitest him?

Psa 8:5 For thou hast made him a little lower than the angels, and hast crowned him with glory and honour.

Hbr 2:3 How shall we escape, if we neglect so great salvation; which at the first began to be spoken by the Lord, and was confirmed unto us by them that heard [him];

Hbr 2:4 God also bearing [them] witness, both with signs and wonders, and with divers miracles, and gifts of the Holy Ghost, according to his own will?

Hbr 2:5 For unto the angels hath he not put in subjection the world to come, whereof we speak.

Hbr 2:6 But one in a certain place testified, saying, What is man, that thou art mindful of him? or the son of man, that thou visitest him?

Hbr 2:7 Thou madest him a little lower than the angels; thou crownedst him with glory and honour, and didst set him over the works of thy hands:

Hbr 2:8 Thou hast put all things in subjection under his feet. For in that he put all in subjection under him, he left nothing [that is] not put under him. But now we see not yet all things put under him.

Hbr 2:9 But we see Jesus, who was made a little lower than the angels for the suffering of death, crowned with glory and honour; that he by the grace of God should taste death for every man.

Hbr 2:10 For it became him, for whom [are] all things, and by whom [are] all things, in bringing many sons unto glory, to make the captain of their salvation perfect through sufferings.

Hbr 2:11 For both he that sanctifieth and they who are sanctified [are] all of one: for which cause he is not ashamed to call them brethren,

Hbr 2:12 Saying, I will declare thy name unto my brethren, in the midst of the church will I sing praise unto thee.

Hbr 2:13 And again, I will put my trust in him. And again, Behold I and the children which God hath given me.

Hbr 2:14 Forasmuch then as the children are partakers of flesh and blood, he also himself likewise took part of the same; that through death he might destroy him that had the power of death, that is, the devil;

Hbr 2:15 And deliver them who through fear of death were all their lifetime subject to bondage.

Hbr 2:16 For verily he took not on [him the nature of] angels; but he took on [him] the seed of Abraham.

Hbr 2:17 Wherefore in all things it behoved him to be made like unto [his] brethren, that he might be a merciful and faithful high priest in things [pertaining] to God, to make reconciliation for the sins of the people.

Hbr 2:18 For in that he himself hath suffered being tempted, he is able to succour them that are tempted.

Mat 20:22 But Jesus answered and said, Ye know not what ye ask. Are ye able to drink of the cup that I shall drink of, and to be baptized with the baptism that I am baptized with? They say unto him, We are able.

Mat 20:23 And he saith unto them, Ye shall drink indeed of my cup, and be baptized with the baptism that I am baptized with: but to sit on my right hand, and on my left, is not mine to give, but [it shall be given to them] for whom it is prepared of my Father.

Mar 10:38 But Jesus said unto them, Ye know not what ye ask: can ye drink of the cup that I drink of? and be baptized with the baptism that I am baptized with?

Mar 10:39 And they said unto him, We can. And Jesus said unto them, Ye shall indeed drink of the cup that I drink of; and with the baptism that I am baptized withal shall ye be baptized:

1Pe 4:1 Forasmuch then as Christ hath suffered for us in the flesh, arm yourselves likewise with the same mind: for he that hath suffered in the flesh hath ceased from sin;

1Pe 4:2 That he no longer should live the rest of [his] time in the flesh to the lusts of men, but to the will of God.

1Pe 4:3 For the time past of [our] life may suffice us to have wrought the will of the Gentiles, when we walked in lasciviousness, lusts, excess of wine, revellings, banquetings, and abominable idolatries:

1Pe 4:4 Wherein they think it strange that ye run not with [them] to the same excess of riot, speaking evil of [you]:

1Pe 4:5 Who shall give account to him that is ready to judge the quick and the dead.

1Pe 4:6 For for this cause was the gospel preached also to them that are dead, that they might be judged according to men in the flesh, but live according to God in the spirit.

1Pe 4:7 But the end of all things is at hand: be ye therefore sober, and watch unto prayer.

1Pe 4:8 And above all things have fervent charity among yourselves: for charity shall cover the multitude of sins.

1Pe 4:9 Use hospitality one to another without grudging.

The body of Christ, the church consists of humans in the image of God, the manifestation of His Word, fulfilling His expectation. God then is human being as He declared in the beginning. God decided to create humans in His image.

Phl 2:5 Let this mind be in you, which was also in Christ Jesus:
Phl 2:6 Who, being in the form of God, thought it not robbery to be equal with God:
Phl 2:7 But made himself of no reputation, and took upon him the form of a servant, and was made in the likeness of men:
Phl 2:8 And being found in fashion as a man, he humbled himself, and became obedient unto death, even the death of the cross.
Phl 2:9 Wherefore God also hath highly exalted him, and given him a name which is above every name:
Phl 2:10 That at the name of Jesus every knee should bow, of [things] in heaven, and [things] in earth, and [things] under the earth;
Phl 2:11 And [that] every tongue should confess that Jesus Christ [is] Lord, to the glory of God the Father.
Isa 45:23 I have sworn by myself, the word is gone out of my mouth [in] righteousness, and shall not return, That unto me every knee shall bow, every tongue shall swear.
Act 4:8 Then Peter, filled with the Holy Ghost, said unto them, Ye rulers of the people, and elders of Israel,
Act 4:9 If we this day be examined of the good deed done to the impotent man, by what means he is made whole;
Act 4:10 Be it known unto you all, and to all the people of Israel, that by the name of Jesus Christ of Nazareth, whom ye crucified, whom God raised from

the dead, [even] by him doth this man stand here before you whole.

Act 4:11 This is the stone which was set at nought of you builders, which is become the head of the corner.

Act 4:12 Neither is there salvation in any other: for there is none other name under heaven given among men, whereby we must be saved.

Jhn 4:34 Jesus saith unto them, My meat is to do the will of him that sent me, and to finish his work.

Jhn 4:35 Say not ye, There are yet four months, and [then] cometh harvest? behold, I say unto you, Lift up your eyes, and look on the fields; for they are white already to harvest.

Jhn 4:36 And he that reapeth receiveth wages, and gathereth fruit unto life eternal: that both he that soweth and he that reapeth may rejoice together.

Jhn 4:37 And herein is that saying true, One soweth, and another reapeth.

Jhn 4:38 I sent you to reap that whereon ye bestowed no labour: other men laboured, and ye are entered into their labours.

Rom 13:11 And that, knowing the time, that now [it is] high time to awake out of sleep: for now [is] our salvation nearer than when we believed.

Rom 13:12 The night is far spent, the day is at hand: let us therefore cast off the works of darkness, and let us put on the armour of light.

Rom 13:13 Let us walk honestly, as in the day; not in rioting and drunkenness, not in chambering and wantonness, not in strife and envying.

Rom 13:14 But put ye on the Lord Jesus Christ, and make not provision for the flesh, to [fulfil] the lusts [thereof].

Adam and Eve succumbed to heresy. God warned Adam that if he ate the fruit, he would know death. God's word, his warning, proved true in Adam and still with their descendants, with us today. The first occurrence of any concept is severe until familiarity adjusts our acceptance. Our tolerance of sin is our damnation. It is not the image of God.

Pro 8:36 But he that sinneth against me wrongeth his own soul: all they that hate me love death.
Mat 25:44 Then shall they also answer him, saying, Lord, when saw we thee an hungred, or athirst, or a stranger, or naked, or sick, or in prison, and did not minister unto thee?
Mat 25:45 Then shall he answer them, saying, Verily I say unto you, Inasmuch as ye did [it] not to one of the least of these, ye did [it] not to me.
Mat 25:46 And these shall go away into everlasting punishment: but the righteous into life eternal.
Isa 1:18 Come now, and let us reason together, saith the LORD: though your sins be as scarlet, they shall be as white as snow; though they be red like crimson, they shall be as wool.

Moses exhorted the people to choose God.

Deu 30:19 I call heaven and earth to record this day against you, [that] I have set before you life and death, blessing and cursing: therefore choose life, that both thou and thy seed may live:
Act 28:23 And when they had appointed him a day, there came many to him into [his] lodging; to whom he expounded and testified the kingdom of God, persuading them concerning Jesus, both out of the law of Moses, and [out of] the prophets, from morning till evening.
Act 28:24 And some believed the things which were spoken, and some believed not.
Act 28:25 And when they agreed not among themselves, they departed, after that Paul had spoken

one word, Well spake the Holy Ghost by Esaias the prophet unto our fathers,

Act 28:26 Saying, Go unto this people, and say, Hearing ye shall hear, and shall not understand; and seeing ye shall see, and not perceive:

Act 28:27 For the heart of this people is waxed gross, and their ears are dull of hearing, and their eyes have they closed; lest they should see with [their] eyes, and hear with [their] ears, and understand with [their] heart, and should be converted, and I should heal them.

Act 28:28 Be it known therefore unto you, that the salvation of God is sent unto the Gentiles, and [that] they will hear it.

Act 28:29 And when he had said these words, the Jews departed, and had great reasoning among themselves.

Act 28:30 And Paul dwelt two whole years in his own hired house, and received all that came in unto him,

Act 28:31 Preaching the kingdom of God, and teaching those things which concern the Lord Jesus Christ, with all confidence, no man forbidding him.

Our lives will come to an end but we have a promise.

Jhn 3:16 For God so loved the world, that he gave his only begotten Son, that whosoever believeth in him should not perish, but have everlasting life.

Jhn 3:36 He that believeth on the Son hath everlasting life: and he that believeth not the Son shall not see life; but the wrath of God abideth on him.

Jhn 6:47 Verily, verily, I say unto you, he that believeth on Me hath everlasting life.

Mat 19:29 and every one that hath forsaken houses, or brethren, or sisters, or father, or mother, or wife, or children, or lands, for my name's sake, shall receive an hundredfold, and shall inherit everlasting life.

1Cr 2:9 But as it is written, Eye hath not seen, nor ear heard, neither have entered into the heart of man, the things which God hath prepared for them that love him.
1Cr 2:10 But God hath revealed [them] unto us by his Spirit: for the Spirit searcheth all things, yea, the deep things of God.
Isa 64:4 For since the beginning of the world [men] have not heard, nor perceived by the ear, neither hath the eye seen, O God, beside thee, [what] he hath prepared for him that waiteth for him.
Isa 64:5 Thou meetest him that rejoiceth and worketh righteousness, [those that] remember thee in thy ways: behold, thou art wroth; for we have sinned: in those is continuance, and we shall be saved.
Isa 64:6 But we are all as an unclean [thing], and all our righteousnesses [are] as filthy rags; and we all do fade as a leaf; and our iniquities, like the wind, have taken us away.
Isa 64:7 And [there is] none that calleth upon thy name, that stirreth up himself to take hold of thee: for thou hast hid thy face from us, and hast consumed us, because of our iniquities.
Isa 64:8 But now, O LORD, thou [art] our father; we [are] the clay, and thou our potter; and we all [are] the work of thy hand.
Isa 64:9 Be not wroth very sore, O LORD, neither remember iniquity for ever: behold, see, we beseech thee, we [are] all thy people.

Chapter 12
Peter by the Way

Consider Peter for a moment. He stumbled about early in his walk. He was told, "Get behind Me Satan!" He clearly missed the moment atop the Mount of Transfiguration as he blundered, "Lord, it is good for us to be here; if You wish, let us make here three tabernacles: one for You, one for Moses, and one for Elijah." Another time he asked, "Lord, how often shall my brother sin against me, and I forgive him? up to seven times?" He noted elsewhere that the cursed fig tree had withered. Peter also said, "You shall never wash my feet!" Jesus answered him, "If I do not wash you, you have no part with Me." It was Peter who cut off the right ear of the servant Malchus who was with those who came to arrest Jesus. Without realizing his time of trial, three times he denied Jesus in the high priest's palace. Still after participating in great moments of the Holy Spirit he separated himself with Jews who arrived at a feast which scandalized his gentile hosts.

Phl 3:11 If by any means I might attain unto the resurrection of the dead.
Phl 3:12 Not as though I had already attained, either were already perfect: but I follow after, if that I may apprehend that for which also I am apprehended of Christ Jesus.
Phl 3:13 Brethren, I count not myself to have apprehended: but [this] one thing [I do], forgetting those things which are behind, and reaching forth unto those things which are before,
Phl 3:14 I press toward the mark for the prize of the high calling of God in Christ Jesus.
2Cr 4:7 But we have this treasure in earthen vessels, that the excellency of the power may be of God, and not of us.
Luk 22:31 And the Lord said, Simon, Simon, behold, Satan hath desired [to have] you, that he may sift [you] as wheat:

Luk 22:32 But I have prayed for thee, that thy faith fail not: and when thou art converted, strengthen thy brethren.

Associated with his missteps, people do not refer to Peter with the phrase, "walk on water", but he is the only other human who did. Peter ran with John to the empty tomb. Peter was quick to follow his heart, was embarrassingly hasty, refreshingly innocent and young at heart. This trait also put him at some of the greatest moments of the Holy Spirit.

Mat 16:16 And Simon Peter answered and said, Thou art the Christ, the Son of the living God.
Mat 16:17 And Jesus answered and said unto him, Blessed art thou, Simon Barjona: for flesh and blood hath not revealed [it] unto thee, but my Father which is in heaven.
Mat 16:18 And I say also unto thee, That thou art Peter, and upon this rock I will build my church; and the gates of hell shall not prevail against it.
Mat 16:19 And I will give unto thee the keys of the kingdom of heaven: and whatsoever thou shalt bind on earth shall be bound in heaven: and whatsoever thou shalt loose on earth shall be loosed in heaven.

Act 2:14 But Peter, standing up with the eleven, lifted up his voice, and said unto them, Ye men of Judaea, and all [ye] that dwell at Jerusalem, be this known unto you, and hearken to my words:
Act 2:32 This Jesus hath God raised up, whereof we all are witnesses.
Act 2:33 Therefore being by the right hand of God exalted, and having received of the Father the promise of the Holy Ghost, he hath shed forth this, which ye now see and hear.
Act 2:37 Now when they heard [this], they were pricked in their heart, and said unto Peter and to the

rest of the apostles, Men [and] brethren, what shall we do?

Act 2:38 Then Peter said unto them, Repent, and be baptized every one of you in the name of Jesus Christ for the remission of sins, and ye shall receive the gift of the Holy Ghost.

Act 2:39 For the promise is unto you, and to your children, and to all that are afar off, [even] as many as the Lord our God shall call.

Act 3:6 Then Peter said, Silver and gold have I none; but such as I have give I thee: In the name of Jesus Christ of Nazareth rise up and walk.

Act 4:7 And when they had set them in the midst, they asked, By what power, or by what name, have ye done this?

Act 4:8 Then Peter, filled with the Holy Ghost, said unto them, Ye rulers of the people, and elders of Israel,

Act 4:9 If we this day be examined of the good deed done to the impotent man, by what means he is made whole;

Act 4:10 Be it known unto you all, and to all the people of Israel, that by the name of Jesus Christ of Nazareth, whom ye crucified, whom God raised from the dead, [even] by him doth this man stand here before you whole.

Act 4:11 This is the stone which was set at nought of you builders, which is become the head of the corner.

Act 4:12 Neither is there salvation in any other: for there is none other name under heaven given among men, whereby we must be saved.

Act 9:37 And it came to pass in those days, that she was sick, and died: whom when they had washed, they laid [her] in an upper chamber.

Act 9:40 But Peter put them all forth, and kneeled down, and prayed; and turning [him] to the body said,

Tabitha, arise. And she opened her eyes: and when she saw Peter, she sat up.
Act 10:44 While Peter yet spake these words, the Holy Ghost fell on all them which heard the word.
Act 10:45 And they of the circumcision which believed were astonished, as many as came with Peter, because that on the Gentiles also was poured out the gift of the Holy Ghost.

Act 12:7 And, behold, the angel of the Lord came upon [him], and a light shined in the prison: and he smote Peter on the side, and raised him up, saying, Arise up quickly. And his chains fell off from [his] hands.
Act 12:11 And when Peter was come to himself, he said, Now I know of a surety, that the Lord hath sent his angel, and hath delivered me out of the hand of Herod, and [from] all the expectation of the people of the Jews.

Notice Peter's transition from everyday human to a man for and of God occurs despite his human weaknesses. Peter confirms Jesus' words in Luke 22:32 by strengthening us still today through his exposure to and life with and for Jesus. Peter exhorts us now from within the kingdom to work through our weaknesses to the high calling of God.

1Pe 1:7 That the trial of your faith, being much more precious than of gold that perisheth, though it be tried with fire, might be found unto praise and honour and glory at the appearing of Jesus Christ:
Eph 4:13 Till we all come in the unity of the faith, and of the knowledge of the Son of God, unto a perfect man, unto the measure of the stature of the fulness of Christ:
Eph 4:14 That we [henceforth] be no more children, tossed to and fro, and carried about with every wind of

doctrine, by the sleight of men, [and] cunning craftiness, whereby they lie in wait to deceive;

Rom 8:12 Therefore, brethren, we are debtors, not to the flesh, to live after the flesh.

Rom 8:13 For if ye live after the flesh, ye shall die: but if ye through the Spirit do mortify the deeds of the body, ye shall live.

Rom 8:14 For as many as are led by the Spirit of God, they are the sons of God.

Rom 8:15 For ye have not received the spirit of bondage again to fear; but ye have received the Spirit of adoption, whereby we cry, Abba, Father.

Rom 8:16 The Spirit itself beareth witness with our spirit, that we are the children of God:

1Jo 4:2 Hereby know ye the Spirit of God: Every spirit that confesseth that Jesus Christ is come in the flesh is of God:

1Jo 4:3 And every spirit that confesseth not that Jesus Christ is come in the flesh is not of God: and this is that [spirit] of antichrist, whereof ye have heard that it should come; and even now already is it in the world.

1Jo 4:4 Ye are of God, little children, and have overcome them: because greater is he that is in you, than he that is in the world.

1Jo 4:5 They are of the world: therefore speak they of the world, and the world heareth them.

1Jo 4:6 We are of God: he that knoweth God heareth us; he that is not of God heareth not us. Hereby know we the spirit of truth, and the spirit of error.

1Jo 4:7 Beloved, let us love one another: for love is of God; and every one that loveth is born of God, and knoweth God.

1Jo 4:8 He that loveth not knoweth not God; for God is love.

1Jo 4:9 In this was manifested the love of God toward us, because that God sent his only begotten Son into the world, that we might live through him.

1Jo 4:10 Herein is love, not that we loved God, but that he loved us, and sent his Son [to be] the propitiation for our sins.

1Jo 4:11 Beloved, if God so loved us, we ought also to love one another.

1Jo 4:12 No man hath seen God at any time. If we love one another, God dwelleth in us, and his love is perfected in us.

1Jo 4:13 Hereby know we that we dwell in him, and he in us, because he hath given us of his Spirit.

1Jo 4:14 And we have seen and do testify that the Father sent the Son [to be] the Saviour of the world.

1Jo 4:15 Whosoever shall confess that Jesus is the Son of God, God dwelleth in him, and he in God.

1Jo 4:16 And we have known and believed the love that God hath to us. God is love; and he that dwelleth in love dwelleth in God, and God in him.

1Jo 4:17 Herein is our love made perfect, that we may have boldness in the day of judgment: because as he is, so are we in this world.

1Jo 4:18 There is no fear in love; but perfect love casteth out fear: because fear hath torment. He that feareth is not made perfect in love.

1Jo 4:19 We love him, because he first loved us.

2Cr 5:21 For he hath made him [to be] sin for us, who knew no sin; that we might be made the righteousness of God in him.

Who we are is evidenced throughout biblical scripture. We were not forsaken at the tragedy of Genesis. The fall and falls throughout Genesis and the Old and New Testaments reveal the violence and incongruity of human existence without the Spirit of God.

Physical elements are pushed and pulled to express human thought and will but then too, the physical pushes back. We are constrained in the physical, we hunger; we strive against the elements and disease. Human compassion and sharing surpass hardships yet are found wanting due to selfishness, pride, envy and strife. Godlike qualities fall away where God is denied. Our thoughts yearn for supernatural ability and existence. Contemporary societies do relieve us from coarse physical conditions, impairments and diseases but only conditionally. Many people live apart from the comfort and luxury of these shining societies. All the modern accomplishments subsist subject to an unsettled truce. Eras of peace are necessary for human creations of health, utility and beauty but even along with the greatest expressions of human accomplishment there are others who resent, suppress murder and hold captive. Within the great societies we also find human castoffs and numbers of neglected and depressed people. The image and likeness of God was lost at the Garden in Eden. The descendants of flesh and blood propagate the sin of Adam and Eve. Humanism is rebellion against God; human will denying God. Tragically, human history attests to self inflicted harm and mayhem in life apart from God.

1Cr 10:11 Now all these things happened unto them for ensamples: and they are written for our admonition, upon whom the ends of the world are come.
2Cr 6:2 (For he saith, I have heard thee in a time accepted, and in the day of salvation have I succoured thee: behold, now [is] the accepted time; behold, now [is] the day of salvation.)
Col 1:9 For this cause we also, since the day we heard [it], do not cease to pray for you, and to desire that ye might be filled with the knowledge of his will in all wisdom and spiritual understanding;
Col 1:10 That ye might walk worthy of the Lord unto all pleasing, being fruitful in every good work, and increasing in the knowledge of God;
Col 1:11 Strengthened with all might, according to his glorious power, unto all patience and longsuffering with joyfulness;

Col 1:12 Giving thanks unto the Father, which hath made us meet to be partakers of the inheritance of the saints in light:

Col 1:13 Who hath delivered us from the power of darkness, and hath translated [us] into the kingdom of his dear Son:

Col 1:14 In whom we have redemption through his blood, [even] the forgiveness of sins:

Col 1:15 Who is the image of the invisible God, the firstborn of every creature:

Col 1:16 For by him were all things created, that are in heaven, and that are in earth, visible and invisible, whether [they be] thrones, or dominions, or principalities, or powers: all things were created by him, and for him:

Col 1:17 And he is before all things, and by him all things consist.

Col 1:18 And he is the head of the body, the church: who is the beginning, the firstborn from the dead; that in all [things] he might have the preeminence.

Col 1:19 For it pleased [the Father] that in him should all fulness dwell;

Col 1:20 And, having made peace through the blood of his cross, by him to reconcile all things unto Himself; by Him, [I say], whether [they be] things in earth, or things in heaven.

Col 1:21 And you, that were sometime alienated and enemies in [your] mind by wicked works, yet now hath He reconciled

Col 1:22 In the body of his flesh through death, to present you holy and unblameable and unreproveable in His sight:

Col 1:23 If ye continue in the faith grounded and settled, and [be] not moved away from the hope of the gospel, which ye have heard, [and] which was preached to every creature which is under heaven; whereof I Paul am made a minister;

1Cr 9:24 Know ye not that they which run in a race run all, but one receiveth the prize? So run, that ye may obtain.
1Cr 9:25 And every man that striveth for the mastery is temperate in all things. Now they [do it] to obtain a corruptible crown; but we an incorruptible.
1Cr 9:26 I therefore so run, not as uncertainly; so fight I, not as one that beateth the air:
1Cr 9:27 But I keep under my body, and bring [it] into subjection: lest that by any means, when I have preached to others, I myself should be a castaway.

Overcoming, the fruit of life aligned with and full of The Lamb

Hbr 3:6 But Christ as a son over his own house; whose house are we, if we hold fast the confidence and the rejoicing of the hope firm unto the end.
Hbr 3:7 Wherefore (as the Holy Ghost saith, To day if ye will hear his voice,
Hbr 3:8 Harden not your hearts, as in the provocation, in the day of temptation in the wilderness:
Hbr 3:9 When your fathers tempted me, proved me, and saw my works forty years.
Hbr 3:10 Wherefore I was grieved with that generation, and said, They do alway err in [their] heart; and they have not known my ways.
Hbr 3:11 So I sware in my wrath, They shall not enter into my rest.)
Hbr 3:12 Take heed, brethren, lest there be in any of you an evil heart of unbelief, in departing from the living God.
Hbr 3:13 But exhort one another daily, while it is called today; lest any of you be hardened through the deceitfulness of sin.

Hbr 3:14 For we are made partakers of Christ, if we hold the beginning of our confidence stedfast unto the end;

Hbr 3:15 While it is said, today if ye will hear his voice, harden not your hearts, as in the provocation.

Hbr 3:16 For some, when they had heard, did provoke: howbeit not all that came out of Egypt by Moses.

Hbr 3:17 But with whom was he grieved forty years? [was it] not with them that had sinned, whose carcases fell in the wilderness?

Hbr 3:18 And to whom sware he that they should not enter into his rest, but to them that believed not?

Hbr 3:19 So we see that they could not enter in because of unbelief.

2Pe 2:20 For if after they have escaped the pollutions of the world through the knowledge of the Lord and Saviour Jesus Christ, they are again entangled therein, and overcome, the latter end is worse with them than the beginning.

2Pe 2:21 For it had been better for them not to have known the way of righteousness, than, after they have known [it], to turn from the holy commandment delivered unto them.

Hbr 10:35 Cast not away therefore your confidence, which hath great recompence of reward.

Hbr 10:36 For ye have need of patience, that, after ye have done the will of God, ye might receive the promise.

Hbr 10:37 For yet a little while, and he that shall come will come, and will not tarry.

Hbr 10:38 Now the just shall live by faith: but if [any man] draw back, my soul shall have no pleasure in him.

Hbr 10:39 But we are not of them who draw back unto perdition; but of them that believe to the saving of the soul.

Rom 11:22 Behold therefore the goodness and severity of God: on them which fell, severity; but toward thee, goodness, if thou continue in [his] goodness: otherwise thou also shalt be cut off.

Rev 2:2 I know thy works, and thy labour, and thy patience, and how thou canst not bear them which are evil: and thou hast tried them which say they are apostles, and are not, and hast found them liars:

Rev 2:3 And hast borne, and hast patience, and for my name's sake hast laboured, and hast not fainted.

Rev 2:4 Nevertheless I have [somewhat] against thee, because thou hast left thy first love.

Rev 2:5 Remember therefore from whence thou art fallen, and repent, and do the first works; or else I will come unto thee quickly, and will remove thy candlestick out of his place, except thou repent.

Rev 2:25 But that which ye have [already] hold fast till I come.

Rev 12:12 Therefore rejoice, [ye] heavens, and ye that dwell in them. Woe to the inhabiters of the earth and of the sea! for the devil is come down unto you, having great wrath, because he knoweth that he hath but a short time.

Psa 32:2 Blessed [is] the man unto whom the LORD imputeth not iniquity, and in whose spirit [there is] no guile.

Psa 32:5 I acknowledged my sin unto thee, and mine iniquity have I not hid. I said, I will confess my transgressions unto the LORD; and thou forgavest the iniquity of my sin. Selah.

1Jo 1:5 This then is the message which we have heard of him, and declare unto you, that God is light, and in him is no darkness at all.

1Jo 1:6 If we say that we have fellowship with him, and walk in darkness, we lie, and do not the truth:

1Jo 1:7 But if we walk in the light, as he is in the light, we have fellowship one with another, and the blood of Jesus Christ his Son cleanseth us from all sin.

1Jo 1:8 If we say that we have no sin, we deceive ourselves, and the truth is not in us.

1Jo 1:9 If we confess our sins, he is faithful and just to forgive us [our] sins, and to cleanse us from all unrighteousness.

1Jo 1:10 If we say that we have not sinned, we make him a liar, and his word is not in us.

2Ti 1:9 Who hath saved us, and called [us] with an holy calling, not according to our works, but according to his own purpose and grace, which was given us in Christ Jesus before the world began,

Hbr 8:12 For I will be merciful to their unrighteousness, and their sins and their iniquities will I remember no more.

Psa 104:35 Let the sinners be consumed out of the earth, and let the wicked be no more. Bless thou the LORD, O my soul. Praise ye the LORD.

Deu 32:39 See now that I, [even] I, [am] he, and [there is] no god with me: I kill, and I make alive; I wound, and I heal: neither [is there any] that can deliver out of my hand.

Deu 32:40 For I lift up my hand to heaven, and say, I live for ever.

Isa 45:21 Tell ye, and bring [them] near; yea, let them take counsel together: who hath declared this from ancient time? [who] hath told it from that time? [have] not I the LORD? and [there is] no God else beside me; a just God and a Saviour; [there is] none beside me.

Isa 45:22 Look unto me, and be ye saved, all the ends of the earth: for I [am] God, and [there is] none else.

Eph 2:10 For we are his workmanship, created in Christ Jesus unto good works, which God hath before ordained that we should walk in them.

2Ti 1:10 But is now made manifest by the appearing of our Saviour Jesus Christ, who hath abolished death, and hath brought life and immortality to light through the gospel:

Eph 3:9 And to make all [men] see what [is] the fellowship of the mystery, which from the beginning of the world hath been hid in God, who created all things by Jesus Christ:

Col 1:16 For by him were all things created, that are in heaven, and that are in earth, visible and invisible, whether [they be] thrones, or dominions, or principalities, or powers: all things were created by him, and for him:

Rev 4:11 Thou art worthy, O Lord, to receive glory and honour and power: for thou hast created all things, and for thy pleasure they are and were created.

Rev 22:6 And he said unto me, These sayings [are] faithful and true: and the Lord God of the holy prophets sent his angel to shew unto his servants the things which must shortly be done.

Rev 22:16 I Jesus have sent mine angel to testify unto you these things in the churches. I am the root and the offspring of David, [and] the bright and morning star.

Gen 1:28 And God blessed them, and God said unto them, Be fruitful, and multiply, and replenish the earth, and subdue it: and have dominion over the fish of the sea, and over the fowl of the air, and over every living thing that moveth upon the earth.

Gen 1:31 And God saw every thing that he had made, and, behold, [it was] very good. And the evening and the morning were the sixth day.

1Jo 5:4 For whatsoever is born of God overcometh the world: and this is the victory that overcometh the world, [even] our faith.

1Jo 5:5 Who is he that overcometh the world, but he that believeth that Jesus is the Son of God?

Rev 2:7 He that hath an ear, let him hear what the Spirit saith unto the churches; To him that overcometh will I give to eat of the tree of life, which is in the midst of the paradise of God.

Rev 2:11 He that hath an ear, let him hear what the Spirit saith unto the churches; He that overcometh shall not be hurt of the second death.

Rev 2:17 He that hath an ear, let him hear what the Spirit saith unto the churches; To him that overcometh will I give to eat of the hidden manna, and will give him a white stone, and in the stone a new name written, which no man knoweth saving he that receiveth [it].

Rev 2:26 And he that overcometh, and keepeth my works unto the end, to him will I give power over the nations:

Rev 3:5 He that overcometh, the same shall be clothed in white raiment; and I will not blot out his name out of the book of life, but I will confess his name before my Father, and before his angels.

Rev 3:12 Him that overcometh will I make a pillar in the temple of my God, and he shall go no more out: and I will write upon him the name of my God, and the name of the city of my God, [which is] new Jerusalem, which cometh down out of heaven from my God: and [I will write upon him] my new name.

Rev 3:21 To him that overcometh will I grant to sit with me in my throne, even as I also overcame, and am set down with my Father in his throne.

Rev 21:7 He that overcometh shall inherit all things; and I will be his God, and he shall be my son.

Rev 22:17 And the Spirit and the bride say, Come. And let him that heareth say, Come. And let him that is athirst come. And whosoever will, let him take the water of life freely.

Made in the USA
Charleston, SC
30 December 2011